ISBN 978-0-267-00712-7
PIBN 10806781

THE YEAR OF PRAISE

Being Hymns, with Tunes, for the Sundays and Holidays of the Year

INTENDED FOR USE IN CANTERBURY CATHEDRAL, AND ADAPTED FOR CATHEDRAL
AND PARISH CHURCHES GENERALLY

EDITED BY HENRY ALFORD, D.D.

DEAN OF CANTERBURY

Assisted in the Musical Part by ROBERT HAKE, M.A., Precentor, and
THOMAS EVANCE JONES, Organist, of Canterbury Cathedral

ALEXANDER STRAHAN, PUBLISHER

56, LUDGATE HILL, LONDON

1867

London :
Henderson, Rait, and Fenton, General Printers,
23, Berners Street, Oxford Street.

PREFACE.

THE *Year of Praise* is primarily intended for use in Canterbury Cathedral. But it has also been the wish of the Editors to adapt it to the requirements of Parish Churches generally. It is for this latter purpose that Four Hymns have been provided for each Sunday and principal Holiday, whereas Cathedral use needed but two.

The first of these four Hymns in every case is chosen with a view to the principal subject of the day, and is intended to serve as an Introit, *i.e.*, to be sung when the clergy go up to the Lord's Table for the Communion Service. At this time, it has been usual, in our Cathedral, to sing a portion of the Sanctus from the Communion Service itself: an unauthorized and negligent habit, coming down to us from days when weekly Communion was disused. The introduction of the Sanctus in this place is now simply tautological, as it occurs again during the celebration of the Holy Communion. It is proposed, therefore, to discontinue the practice, and instead of it to sing, without giving out, the Introit, or first Hymn for the day. It is presumed that in case the book is used in any Parish Churches, the same practice will probably be followed. The other three Hymns for each Sunday and principal Holiday are chosen for the most part to suit either the main or collateral subjects of the day; or if, as on some of the Sundays after Epiphany and Trinity, no subject appeared sufficiently prominent, recourse has been had to Hymns of more general import. For the use of such Churches as need more than four Hymns for each Sunday, and of those clergymen who may wish sometimes to suit particular occasions, as *e.g.* that of a Festival falling on a Sunday, an Index of Subjects has been appended, by means of which additional Hymns may be found in other portions of the book, suitable for the season, or for the subject of the sermon, or for the occasion required.

It is intended that our second Hymn in the Cathedral should be sung between the Prayers and the Sermon in the Afternoon Service, where now the organist plays *a short voluntary. It will* be ordinarily chosen from among the three remaining

Hymns for the day; or, if occasion require, from other parts of the book; and will be given out, as the anthems are.

The practice of concluding every Hymn with an "Amen" has not been followed in this book. The tune being complete in itself, no such termination is musically required; and the sense of the concluding verse not always admitting of the addition, incongruities are frequently produced by it.

It remains that we speak of our obligations to those Hymn writers and Composers who have allowed us the use of their words and tunes, or have been good enough to write specially for us.

For permission to make use of their HYMNS, we have to thank MRS. ALEXANDER, DEAN MILMAN, DEAN STANLEY, ARCHDEACON WORDSWORTH, DR. KENNEDY, DR. MONSELL, DR. VAUGHAN, DR. BONAR, the REVS. SIR H. W. BAKER, ABNER BROWN, H. CASWELL, J. W. HEWETT, W. W. HOW, PHIPPS ONSLOW.

The permission to use Hymns 124, 209, and 280, has been purchased of Messrs. LONGMAN, the proprietors of *Lyra Germanica* and *The Chorale Book for England*.

In the matter of TUNES our obligations have been many. First among them we have to acknowledge the gracious kindness of HER MAJESTY THE QUEEN, who has allowed us the use of "Gotha" (Hymn 200), the composition of the lamented PRINCE CONSORT.

The BISHOP OF ARGYLL AND THE ISLES has allowed us to use the tune "Hymn on Heaven," set to Hymns 128 and 325.

The REV. W. H. HAVERGAL has freely allowed us the use of the tunes in his Collections, and of some besides of his own composing.

The REV. DR. MAURICE has also freely allowed us the use of the tunes in his *Choral Harmony*. Of these two last-mentioned permissions we have, as our Index of Tunes will shew, largely availed ourselves.

The venerable Society for the Promotion of Christian Knowledge has, through its secretary the Rev. J. D. Glennie, given us like permission with regard to its Collection.

We have also to acknowledge our obligations to the Dublin Society for the Promotion of Christian Knowledge.

The Editors of Hymns Ancient and Modern have kindly granted us the use of the tunes "*Annue Christe*" (Hymn 129), "Dix" (Hymns 19 and 153), "*Eventide*" (Hymn 318), "Hernlein" (Hymn 29), "Innocents" (Hymns 54,

226, 281 and 301), "Notker" (Hymn 98), "Quam Dilecta" (Hymn 170), "St. Gall" (Hymn 118), "St. Matthias" (Hymns 182 and 317).

The Rev. Sir F. A. G. Ouseley, Bart., Mus. Doc., Professor of Music in the University of Oxford, composed for us "Tenbury" (Hymn 208) and "Eastham" (Hymns 229 and 294).

Herbert S. Oakeley, Esq., Professor of Music in the University of Edinburgh, composed for us "St. Sylvester" (Hymn 27).

The Rev. Henry Allon allowed us the use of "Antioch" (Hymn 219) and "Constance" (Hymn 198), from the *Congregational Psalmist*.

T. D. Acland, Esq., M.P., and Arthur Mills, Esq., Executors of the late A. H. D. Troyte, Esq., allowed us to use his chant to Hymn 162.

To the Rev. R. R. Chope and Dr. Dykes we are indebted for the permission to use "St. Columba" (Hymn 22), composed by the latter.

The Rev. T. Darling permitted us to take from his *Hymns for the Church of England*, Dr. Steggall's arrangement of "Carlisle" (Hymn 131), and Dr. Steggall allowed us the use of his tune "Grosvenor" (Hymn 63) from Dr. Maurice's *Choral Harmony*.

Dr. G. J Elvey composed for us "Dies Iræ" (Hymns 56 and 57) and "Magi" (Hymn 46).

G. Forbes, Esq., Organist of St. Mary's, Marylebone, has permitted us to use "Dowland" (Hymn 319) from his Collection of Tunes.

Dr. Gauntlett allowed us the use of his tunes, "St. Alphege" (Hymn 11) and "St. Albinus" (Hymns 110 and 111).

H. Handel Gear, Esq., Organist of Quebec Chapel, London, has allowed us to print his hitherto unpublished tunes of "Fiat Lux" (Hymn 60) and "Holy Trinity" (Hymn 144).

W. B. Gilbert, Esq., Mus. Bac., Oxon, composed for us "Kidbrook" (Hymn 125, 2).

E. Hake, Esq., composed for us the chant set to Hymn 62.

The Rev. W. J. Hall allowed us to use "Arundel" (Hymn 231) and "Jersey" (Hymn 165).

S. G. Hatherley, Esq., Mus. Bac., Oxon, composed for us "Chara" (Hymn 159).

Dr. Hayne allowed us to use his arrangements of "Eaton" (Hymn 201) and "Potsdam" (Hymns 207 and 253), from the *Merton Tune Book*.

ALBERT HULME, Esq., Choirmaster of St. Thomas's Church, Pendleton, Manchester, allowed us to use his unpublished tune "Redemption" (Hymn 74).

H. S. IRONS, Esq., Organist of Southwell Minster, allowed us to use his tune "Irons" (Hymns 112 and 203).

W. H. LONGHURST, Esq., of Canterbury Cathedral, composed for us "Caen" (Hymn 257, 1), "St. Gabriel" (Hymn 257, 2), "Longhurst" (Hymn 186), and "Newport" (Hymn 205); and also allowed us the use of his tune "Scala Cœli" (Hymn 326).

The REV. W. MERCER allowed us to use the tunes "Baden" (Hymns 3 and 303) and "Upsal" (Hymn 316), from his *Church Psalter and Hymn Book*.

To A. R. REINAGLE, Esq., we are indebted for the use of his tunes, "Ben Rhydding" (Hymn 195), "Ellesmere" (Hymn 307), "Merton College" (Hymns 61, 108, 262 and 295), "Moccas" (Hymn 176), and "Reinagle" (Hymns 187 and 305).

BRINLEY RICHARDS, Esq., gave us permission to adapt his setting of "Herrick's Litany" under the name of "Towy" (Hymn 125, 1), and Messrs. CRAMER & Co. have allowed us to print the same.

JAMES TURLE, Esq., Organist of Westminster Abbey, composed for us "Salve Caput" (Hymn 102).

The permission to use three tunes from the *Chorale Book for England* has been purchased of Messrs. LONGMAN, the proprietors; and the permission to use the tune "Lustra Sex" (Hymn 80), of Messrs. MASTERS & Co.

No endeavour has been spared to trace out the ownership of Hymns and Tunes which are copyright: and it is hoped that none such will be found in this work, for the use of which permission has not been obtained. At the same time such endeavour has proved exceedingly difficult in some cases, and in a few has led to no result. The Editors have, with regard to these last, to throw themselves on the courtesy of the unknown authors or proprietors, and to trust that the permission which, had they known how, they would willingly have asked for, may be kindly given them in the form of pardon for the liberty which they have taken in assuming it.

They also beg to add that any hymns or tunes which are their copyright, are placed freely at the disposal of all who may desire to reprint them.

CANTERBURY, Whitsuntide, 1867.

CONTENTS AND INDEX OF SUBJECTS.

N.B.—The figures printed in thick type indicate the Hymns specially devoted to the subject in this book; the other figures, Hymns having more or less reference to that subject.

ALPHABETICAL INDEX OF HYMNS.

First Lines.	Author or Source.	Tune.
Turn not, O Lord, Thy face from me	... ...	Burford.
Vouchsafe Thy gracious promise, Lord	Cotterill's Collection	Antioch.
We all, O Lord, unrighteous are ...	Christopher Wordsworth ...	French.
We give immortal praise...	Isaac Watts, 1709-1720	Darwell's.
We love the place, O Lord	Bishop Bullock (Songs of the Church, Halifax, U.S., 1854)	Quam Dilecta.
We saw Thee not when Thou didst come...	John Hampden Gurney, 1851...	Colmar.
We sing the praise of Him who died	Thomas Kelly, 1804-1836 ...	Rockingham.
We've no abiding city here	Thomas Kelly, 1804-1836 ...	Chorale 82.
We walk by faith and not by sight	Henry Alford, 1845...	London New.
What are these in bright array ...	James Montgomery...	Seir.
What sinners value, I resign	Isaac Watts, 1709-1720	Tallis's Canon.
Whate'er my God ordains is right ...	Catherine Winkworth (from the German of Rodigast. Lyra Germania) ...	Baden (2nd form).
When Christ the Lord would come on earth	Henry Alford, 1845	Crasselius.
When gathering clouds around I view	Sir Robert Grant, 1839	Magdeburg.
When I survey life's varied scene ...	Anne Steele, 1760	Melrose.
When I survey the wondrous Cross	Isaac Watts, 1709-1720	Saxony.
When in the Lord Jehovah's Name	Henry Alford, 1845...	Baden.
When our heads are bowed with woe	Henry Hart Milman	Lustra Sex.
When, rising from the bed of death	Joseph Addison, 1728	Windsor.
When within sight of danger's hour	Henry Alford, 1845...	Crasselius.
When wounded sore, the stricken heart*	Cecil Frances Alexander, 1858	Martyrs'.
While shepherds watched their flocks by night	Nahum Tate, 1696...	Hayes's 127th.
While with ceaseless course the sun	John Newton, 1779...	Luxemburg.
Who are these like stars appearing...	Frances Eliz. Cox (from the German of Theodor Schenk, d. 1727)	Munden.
Why should I fear the darkest hour	John Newton, 1779	Newport.
Word by God the Father sent ...	Frances Eliz. Cox (from the German. Anon) ... '	Mecklenburgh.
Ye servants of God	Anon	Hanover.
Ye servants of the Lord	Philip Doddridge, 1755	Bochastle.

* By an error, which the reader is requested to correct, "soul" has been printed for "heart" in the body of the book.

METRICAL INDEX OF TUNES.

N.B.—*Those marked with an asterisk * have been composed for or first printed in the present work.*

LONG MEASURE.

Name of Tune.	Composer, or source whence taken.	Harmonised or Arranged by	Hymn.
All Souls	P. Maurice, D.D. Maurice's Choral Harmony ..	P. Maurice, D.D.	93
Altona (or Breslau) ..	Clauderi Psalmodia, 1636 ..	Chiefly Maurice (Choral Harmony)	120
Angelus	J. Scheffler, 1657	James Turle (S.P.C.K. Collection)	314
Arundel	S. Webbe, 1816. From Psalms and Hymns, &c., edited by Rev. W. J. Hall, with Tunes edited by John Foster, 1863	.. ..	231
Babylon Streams ..	Dr. T. Campian, 1600 ..	Chiefly Maurice (Choral Harmony)	64, 241
Bamberg	Bamberg Hymn Book, 1628 ..	James Turle (S.P.C.K. Collection)	92
Bavaria (or Potsdam) ..	Ancient German Choral ..	Rev. W. H. Havergal (O.C.P.)	313
Cannons	Handel, 1742 (Fitzwilliam MSS.)	Chiefly Maurice (Choral Harmony)	321
Carisbrook	Henry Lawes, 1638	R. H. and T. E. J. (editors) ..	199
Chorale 37 (or Gotha) ..	Cantionale Sacrum, 2nd edition. Gotha, 1651	Editors of Chorale Book for England..	113
Chorale 82..	Clauderi Psalmodia, 1630 ..	Editors of Chorale Book for England..	115, 151
Constance	Gothaisches Cautional, 1651 ..	Dr. Gauntlett (Congregational Psalmist)	198
Crasselius (or Winchester New ...	Crasselius, a Lutheran Presbyter, cir. 1650.. ..	Havergal (O.C.P.)	9, 258, 309
Crete	Rev. W. H. Havergal ..	Havergal	272 (2)
Dortmund	Hamburg Choral Book ..	Havergal (O.C.P.) ..	169.
Eisleben	Martin Luther, 1543 ..	Chiefly Maurice (Choral Harmony)	146, 248, 323
Ellesmere	A. R. Reinagle ..	A. R. Reinagle	307
Eppendorf..	C. P. Emmanuel Bach, 1778 ..	Havergal (O.C.P.) ..	139, 306
Freudenberg	Cantarium S. Galli, No. 20 ..	Original Harmony ..	278
Harston	Bishop Turton, 1858 ..	From S.P.C.K. Collection ..	69
Hymnus Eucharisticus (or Chapel Royal, or Magdalene ..	Dr. Rogers, 1660	Magdalen Coll. Oxf. Music Book	89, 174
Leipsic	J. H. Schein, 1631 ..	Partly Maurice (Choral Harmony)	90, 149
Melcombe..	S. Webb, 1812	Maurice (Choral Harmony) ..	45, 175
Notker	Adapted from Cantarium S. Galli ..	W. H. Monk (Hymns Ancient and Modern)	98
Playford (or Salisbury) ..	Playford's Psalter, 1671 ..	Havergal (O.C.P.) ..	270
Prayer	James Turle, 1862 (S.P.C.K. Collection)	James Turle	85
Rockingham	Dr. Miller, 1787	R. H. and T. E. J. ..	5, 104, 293
St. Clement	Maurice's Choral Harmony ..	Chiefly Maurice	76
St. Gall	Adapted from Cantarium S. Galli	W. H. Monk (Hymns Ancient and Modern)	118
Savoy	Guillaume Franc, Geneva, about 1543. So Turle, in S.P.C.K. Collection ..	Chiefly Turle	268, 287, 322

Name of Tune.	Composer, or source whence taken.	Harmonized or Arranged by	Hymn.
Saxony	Ancient German Choral before 1588, Havergal (O.C.P.) ..	Chiefly Havergal	94
Tallis's Canon (or Magdalen)	T. Tallis, from Abp. Parker's Psalter	Reduced from original harmony	238, 312
Tallis's Veni Creator ..	Author unknown	From the Choir books, Canterbury Cathedral ..	138, 272 (½)
Ten Commandments (or Ely, or Magdeburg, or St. Mark) ..	Geneva Psalter, 1562	Havergal (O.C.P.)	136, 311
Waldeck	Ancient German Choral	Havergal (O.C.P.)	273, 308
Wareham	W. Knapp, 1760	Chiefly Maurice	40, 143, 269
Weimar	Ph. E. Bach, 1787	Maurice (Choral Harmony) ..	33, 320
Wise (or Saxony) ..	M. Wise, ob. 1687..	R. H. and T. E. J.	302

COMMON MEASURE.

Name of Tune.	Composer, or source whence taken.	Harmonized or Arranged by	Hymn.
Abbey	Scotch Psalter, 1635		161.
Bedford	W. Wheall, Mus. Bac., 1745 ..	Altered from Maurice (Choral Harmony) ..	23, 157, 222
Bedford (minor) ..	.. ..	Altered from Maurice (Choral Harmony)	83, 286
Bristol	Ravenscroft's Psalter, 1621 ..	Havergal (O.C.P.)	279
Burford	Henry Purcell, 1695	Chiefly Maurice	72, 285, 297
Caithness	Scotch Psalter, 1635.	Havergal (O.C.P.)	289
Carlisle	Ravenscroft's Psalter, 1621 ..	Dr. Steggall (Hymns for the Church of England) ..	131
Chichester (old) ..	Ravenscroft's Psalter, 1621 ..	Havergal (O.C.P.)	189, 239
Colchester..	Playford's Psalter..	Gauntlett (Congregational Psalmist) ..	177
Culross	Scotch Psalter, 1635	Maurice (Choral Harmony) ..	73
Eatington	Dr. Croft, 1700 (From Playford's Divine Companion)	Havergal (O.C.P.)	234
Farrant (or Gloucester)..	Adapted from Richard Farrant, 1585 ..	Havergal (O.C.P.)	324
French (or Dundee) ..	Scotch Psalter		114, 244
Gibbons's St. Matthias ..	Orlando Gibbons, 1623 ..	Havergal (O.C.P.)	53, 180
Gloucester..	Ravenscroft's Psalter, 1621 ..	Chiefly Turle	86, 202
Hayes's 127th ..	Dr. Wm. Hayes		20, 254
Hereford	Playford's Psalter, 1702 ..	R. H. and T. E. J.	47, 218
Howard (or St. Clement's) ..	Dr. Howard, 1762.. ..	Chiefly Maurice (Choral Harmony) ..	252
Irons (or Southwell) ..	H. S. Irons..	H. S. Irons..	112, 203
Kent	Supposed old English tune used in Kent	Havergal (O.C.P.)	247
London New (or Newtown) ..	Scotch Psalter, 1635	Chiefly Havergal (O.C.P.) ..	116, 249
Manchester	Playford's Psalter, 1702 ..	R. H. and T. E. J.	77
Martyrdom (or All Saints)	Hugh Wilson	Altered from Turle (S.P.C.K. Collection) ..	65, 220
Martyrs' (old)	Scotch Psalter, 1611	From S.P.C.K. Collection ..	84, 188
Melrose	Scotch Psalter, 1635	Havergal (O.C.P.)	130
Norwich	Playford's Psalter, 1702 ..	R. H. and T. E. J.	55, 232
Nottingham	Jeremiah Clark, 1700	.. ..	178, 250
Peterborough	Playford's Psalter, 1702 ..	R. H. and T. E. J.	36, 224
Reinagle (or St. Peter's, Oxford) ..	A. R. Reinagle	A. R. Reinagle	187, 305
St. Ann's	Dr. Croft, cir., 1712. By some ascribed to Denby, 1686	From the Choir books, Canterbury Cathedral ..	212, 282
St. David's	Ravenscroft's Psalter, 1621 ..	.. ..	28, 194, 25
St. George (see also Elvey)	Nicolaus Hermann, 1861 ..	T. E. I.	8, 135
St. James	Raphael Courtville, 1580.. ..	Maurice (Choral Harmony) ..	43, 150
St. Mary's..	Dr. Blow, 1708	Chiefly Maurice (Choral Harmony) ..	31, 284
*St. Mildred's	Henry Alford, 1866	T. E. J	260
St. Stephen's (or Nayland)	Rev. W. Jones, 1799	Original Harmony.. ..	181, 304
Salisbury	Ravenscroft's Psalter, 1621 ..	Havergal (O.C.P.)	193
Sunday Tune	Playford's Psalter, 1702 ..	R. H. and T. E. J.	121, 217

Name of Tune.	Composer, or source whence taken.	Harmonized or Arranged by	Hymn.
Tallis's Ordinal (or Veni Creator)	T. Tallis, ar., 1565	Chiefly Havergal (O.C.P.)	52, 274, 288
Winchester (old)	Alison's Psalter, 1599 ..	R. H. and T. E. J.	24, 154
Windsor (or Dundee) ..	Scotch Psalter, 1615; ascribed also to Kirby, 1592; but probably still older ..	Havergal (O.C.P.)	81, 190
York	Scotch Psalter, 1615	Havergal (O.C.P.)	109

DOUBLE COMMON MEASURE.

Richmond	Orlando Gibbons, 1623 ..	Maurice (Choral Harmony) ..	78
St. Matthew ..	Dr. Croft, 1703	R. H. and T. E. J.	96, 283

SHORT MEASURE.

Ben Rhydding	A. R. Reinagle . ..	A. R. Reinagle	195
Bochastle	Henry Alford, 1866 ..	T. E. J.	227, 291
Dort	G. P. Teleman, 1770 ..	Maurice (Choral Harmony) ..	196, 251
Franconia	German melody, cir, 1720	Havergal (O.C.P.)	6, 173
Ludlow	Ravenscroft's Psalter, 1621	Havergal (O.C.P.)	185, 242
Moccas	A. R. Reinagle	A. R. Reinagle	176
Narenza	Ancient chorale from the Cologne Hymn-book	Chiefly Havergal (O.C.P.) ..	163, 261
Potsdam	John Sebastian Bach, 1731	Rev. L. G. Hayne, Mus. D. (From the Merton Tune Book)	207, 253
St. Bride	Dr. Howard, 1780 ..	Maurice (Choral Harmony) ..	184, 298
St. Michael	The Psalter of 1565 ..	Chiefly Maurice (Choral Harmony)	1, 230, 259
St. Peter's	Playford's Psalter, 1702 ..	R. H. and T. E. J.	12, 204
Southwell	Playford's Psalter, 1671 ..	Chiefly Maurice (Choral Harmony)	10
Supplication	T. F. Walmisley, 1853 (from Maurice, Choral Harmony)	.. ..	263
Swabia	Ancient German Melody ..	Havergal (O.C.P.)	156
Tytherton (or Moravia, or Prague) ..	Rev. Joseph West, 1800 ..	Chiefly Maurice (Choral Harmony)	34, 164

DOUBLE SHORT MEASURE.

Old 25th	Day's Psalter, 1563 ..	Chiefly Havergal (O.C.P.) ..	123
Old 34th	Reduced from Dutch Psalter	Chiefly Maurice (Choral Harmony)	7

SEVENS (Three lines).

Paraclete	Crüger, 1666	Altered from Turle (S.P.C.K. Collection)	124

SEVENS (Four lines).

Brasted	From a Chorale by Peter Weimar, about 1780 ..	Turle (S.P.C.K. Collection) ..	256
Delaware	J. Antes	Maurice (Choral Harmony) ..	171
Dix	German	Slightly altered from W. H. Monk (Hymns Ancient and Modern) ..	19, 153
Frankfort	G. Joseph, 1690 ..	Altered from Maurice (Choral Harmony)	95
Gibbons (or Whitehall) ..	Orlando Gibbons, 1623 ..	Partly Maurice (Choral Harmony)	2
Grilfrath (or Ulm) ..	Telemann's Chorale Book, 1730	Havergal (O.C.P.)	38
Hernlein	German	W. H. Monk (Hymns Ancient and Modern) ..	29
Innocents (or Durham) ..	Origin unknown, ascribed by some to S. Webbe, 1806	W. H. Monk (Hymns Ancient and Modern) ..	54, 226, 281, 301
Jersey	Dr. Boyce, 1779	Foster's Tunes (accompanying Rev. W. J. Hall's Psalms and Hymns)	165

Name of Tune.	Composer, or source whence taken.	Harmonised or Arranged by	Hymn.
Lawes (or Shropshire, or Whitehall) ..	Henry Lawes, 1686	Maurice (Choral Harmony) ..	59, 264
Lubeck	Freylinghausen, 1744 ..	Turle (S.P.C.K. Collection) ..	26, 223
Lustra Sex (or Redhead, 47) ..	R. Redhead	R. Redhead	80
Luxemburg	Ancient German Chorale	Havergal (O C.P.)	25, 97
*Magi	Dr. G. J. Elvey, 1866 ..	Dr. G. J. Elvey	46
Minden	German, 1776	Chiefly Maurice (Choral Harmony)	103
Oldenburg..	Ancient German Chorale	Havergal (O C.P.)	245
*Redemption __ ..	Albert Hulme	Albert Hulme	74
St. Columba	Origin unknown; from the Congregational Hymn and Tune Book by the Rev. R. R. Chope	Rev. J. B. Dykes, Mus. Doc. ..	22
*St Thomas	Henry Alford, 1866 ..	T. E. J.	71
Sepher	Havergal (One Hundred Psalm Tunes) ..	Havergal	290
Vienna (or Knecht) ..	J. H. Knecht, 1793	Chiefly Havergal (O.C.P.) ..	37, 142

SEVENS (Four lines, with Hallelujah).

Worgan's (or Easter Hymn)	Dr. Worgan, ob. 1790	.. ..	106

SEVENS (Six lines).

Mayenne	Goudimel, 1565	Maurice (Choral Harmony) ..	91, 215
Nassau	John Rosenmuller, ob. 1686 ..	Maurice (Choral Harmony) ..	35, 152
Presburg	E. Bach	T. E. J.	100
Ratisbon	Werner's New Saxon Chorale Book, Leipsic, 1815 ..	Havergal (O.C.P.)	41, 148, 214, 310
Werner (or Cassell) ..	German	R. H. and T. E. J.	67, 293

SEVENS (Eight lines).

Dowland	Arranged from Dowland.. ..	G. Forbes' Collection of Psalm and Hymn Tunes ..	319
Elvey (or St. George's) ..	Dr. J. G. Elvey	Dr. J. G. Elvey	107, 225, 275
Hamburgh..	J. Schop, 1641	Chiefly Maurice (Choral Harmony)	49, 147
Mayenne	Goudimel, 1565	Maurice (Choral Harmony) ..	30
Mecklenburgh	Freylinghausen, 1704 ..	Maurice (Choral Harmony) ..	160, 267
Seir	Havergal (One Hundred Psalm Tunes) ..	Havergal	265
Vulpius (or Weimar) ..	Melchior Vulpius, 1609 ..	Turle (S.P.C.K. Collection) ..	133, 179
*Warfare	Henry Alford, 1867 ..	T. E. J.	166
Wheatfield..	J. S. Bach, 1688	Chiefly Maurice (Supplement to Choral Harmony) ..	141, 276

SEVENS (Nine lines).

*Dies Iræ	Dr. G. J. Elvey	Dr. G. J. Elvey	56, 57

SEVENS (Ten lines).

Bethlehem Ephratah ..	Mendelssohn, ob. 1846 ..	Mendelssohn	18

12 12 12, 10.

*Holy Trinity	H. Handel Gear	H. Handel Gear	144

10 10, 10 10, 10 10.

Dorchester (or Stockport, or Yorkshire) ..	Dr. Wainright, ob. 1782..	Chiefly from old choir books at Wymeswold, Leicestershire	17

10 10 10 10 10.

Old 124th (or Basle, or Montague) ..	Day's Psalter, 1563	Havergal (O.C.P.)	246

Name of Tune.	Composer, or source whence taken.	Harmonized or Arranged by	Hymn.
	10 10, 10 10.		
Eventide	{ W. H. Monk (Hymns Ancient and Modern) .. .. }	W. H. Monk	318
	10 10, 11 11.		
Hanover	Dr. Croft, ob. 1727	{ Chiefly Turle (S.P.C.K. Collection) .. }	39
Old 104th	Ravenscroft's Psalter, 1621 ..	Chiefly Havergal (O.C.P.) ..	197
	9 8, 9 8, 9 8, 9 8.		
Goudimel (or Eucharistic Hymn) .. }	Goudimel, 1565	Turle (S.P.C.K. Collection) ..	172
	8 8 8 8 8 8.		
Altorf (or Luther's) ..	Luther	Chiefly Hawes	296
	8 8, 8 8, 8 8.		
Angels'	Orlando Gibbons, 1623	Havergal (O.C.P.)	44, 140
Antioch	{ Old Latin, "Veni Sancte Spiritus," adapted by Luther }	{ Dr. Gauntlett (Congregational Psalmist) }	219
Colmar	Michael Gasteritz, before 1544 ..	Havergal (O.C.P.)	192, 240
Eaton	Mywill	Dr. Haine (Merton Tune Book)	201
Magdeburg	Luther	{ Editors of Chorale Book for England .. .. }	211
Mamre	{ Havergal (One Hundred Psalm Tunes) .. .. }	Havergal	277
St. Matthias	{ W. H. Monk (Hymns Ancient and Modern) .. }	W. H. Monk	182, 317
	8 8 8 8 8.		
*Tenebræ	Henry Alford, 1866	T. E. J.	101
	8 8 8 8, 7.		
Baden (or Nuremberg) ..	J. Pachenell, 1690..	{ Rink (from Mercer's Church Psalter and Hymn Book) }	3, 303
	8 8, 8 8, 7, Trochaic.		
*Salve Caput	James Turle, 1866..	James Turle	102
	8 8 8, 6.		
Chestergate	Robert Barnett, 1853 ..	From Maurice (Choral Harmony)	183
Hatherton	Havergal	Havergal	87
*Longhurst	W. H. Longhurst, 1866 ..	W. H. Longhurst	186
	8 8 8, 6, Trochaic.		
*Starcross	Henry Alford, 1866	T. E. J.	48
	8 8 8.		
*Newport	W. H. Longhurst, 1866	W. H. Longhurst	205
	8 8 6, 8 8 6.		
Herrnhutt	Rev. C. Gregor's Collection, 1784	Maurice (Choral Harmony) ..	206
New College	Dr. Wm. Hayes, 1780	Havergal (O.C.P.)	233
	8 7, 8 7.		
Bremen (or Coburg) ..	{ Rev. Joachim Neander, Presbyter of Bremen, 1680 }	Havergal (O.C.P.)	51, 235
Culbach	Tupler's Old Choral Melodies ..	Havergal (O.C.P.)	137
Gotha	H.R.H. Prince Consort ..	The Prince Consort	200
Prague	German Chorale	Havergal (O.C.P.)	127
Tranby	Rev. S. M. Barkworth ..	From Maurice (Choral Harmony)	119, 243
Turnau	Guadam	{ G. W. Torrance (Dublin Church Hymnal) .. }	221

Name of Tune.	Composer, or source whence taken.	Harmonized or Arranged by	Hymn.
	8 7, 8 7, 8 7.		
Göttingen	J. Ch. Bottner, Hanover, 1800 ..	{ Chiefly Maurice (Choral Harmony) .. .. .. }	?
Salzburg (or Benediction, or Corinth, or St. Werbergh's, or Tantum Ergo) ..	Michael Haydn, 1800	Maurice (Choral Harmony) ..	14
	8 7, 8 7, 8 7, 8 7.		
Merton College	A. R. Reinagle	A. R. Reinagle	61, 108, 262, 295
Stuttgart	German	Würtemburg Gesangbuch ..	299
	8 7, 8 7, 8 8, 7.		
Altorf (or Luther's) ..	Luther	Chiefly Hawes	13, 122
	8 7, 8 7, 7 7.		
Cassell	German Chorale	{ Chiefly Maurice (Choral Harmony) }	167, 315
Munden	Collection by C. F. Baker, 1841	Maurice (Choral Harmony) ..	66, 155
	8 7, 8 7, 6 6 6, 7.		
Ein' feste Burg (or Fortress, or Worms)	Luther	{ Partly from the Würtemburg Gesangbuch .. .. }	228
	8 7, 8 7, 4 4, 8 8.		
Baden (2nd form).. ..	J. Pachenell, 1690..	Würtemburg Gesangbuch ..	209
	8 6, 8 6, 8 8.		
Crüger	J. Crüger	R. H.	168
	8 5, 8 5.		
*Quinquagesima	Henry Alford, 1866	T. E. J.	68
	8 4, 8 4, 8 8 8, 4.		
Upsal	{ Mercer's Church Psalter and Hymn Book .. .. }	Goss	316
	7 8, 7 8, and Hallelujah.		
St Albinus	Dr. Gauntlett	Dr. Gauntlett	110, 111
	7 7, 7 7, 7 7, 4.		
*Epiphany	Henry Alford, 1866	T. E. J.	32
	7 7 7, 6.		
*Kidbrook..	W. B. Gilbert, Mus. Bac. ..	W. B. Gilbert	125 (2)
Towy	Brinley Richards	T. E. J.	125 (1)
	7 7 7, 5.		
Dantzick	Reduced from Dr. Filitz.. ..	Maurice (Choral Harmony) ..	16, 88
	7 7, 5, 7 7, 4.		
*Tenbury	{ Rev. Sir F. A. G. Ouseley, Bart, Mus. Doc. .. }	Sir F. A. G. Ouseley	208
	7 6, 7 6.		
Delaware	J. Antes	{ Adapted from Maurice (Choral Harmony) .. .. }	105
Henneberg	Melchior Vulpius, ob. 1616 ..	Maurice (Choral Harmony) ..	271
St. Alphege	Dr. Gauntlett	Dr. Gauntlett	11
	7 6, 7 6, 7 8, 7 6.		
*Musgrove	T. E. Jones, 1866..	T. E. J.	81

Name of Tune.	Composer, or source whence taken.	Harmonized or Arranged by	Hymn.
7 6, 7 6, 7 6, 7 6.			
Ceylon	Leon. Schröter, 1587	Maurice (Choral Harmony) ..	42, 158, 266
*Eastham	Rev. Sir F. A. G. Ouseley, Bart., Mus. Doc. ..	Sir F. A. G. Ouseley	229, 294
Goldbach	Hamburg Chorale Book, Vulpius and C. E. Bach ..	Havergal (O.C.P.)	58, 236
Hymn on Heaven (or Bernard, or Ewing, or St Bede) ..	A. Ewing	A. Ewing	128, 325
Nantes	French Huguenot Hymn ..	Maurice (Choral Harmony) ..	75
Praise (or Prague) ..	Crüger, 1666	G. W. Torrance (Dublin Church Hymnal) ..	216
Teschner (or Missionary Hymn, or Waterford)	Melchior Teschner, 1613.. ..	Turle (S.P.C.K. Collection) ..	70, 132
7 5, 7 5.			
*Caen	W. H. Longhurst, 1866 ..	W. H. Longhurst	257 (1)
*St. Gabriel ..	W. H. Longhurst, 1866 ..	W. H. Longhurst	257 (2)
6 7, 6 7, 6 6 6 6.			
Nun danket alle Gott ..	Joh. Crüger, 1598–1662 ..	Wurtemburg Gesangbuch ..	280
6 6, 6 6,			
*Beaumont	Rev. R. Hake	R. H.	21, 126
Quam Dilecta	The Bishop of Dunedin ..	The Bishop of Dunedin ..	170
*Sursum Corda	Henry Alford, 1866 ..	T. E. J.	134
6 6, 6 6, 6 6, 6 6.			
Annue Christe	From La Feillée	Rev. S. S. Greatheed (Hymns Ancient and Modern)..	129
6 6 6 6, 8 8.			
Alnwick	Dr. Howard, 1762	Chiefly Maurice (Choral Harmony)	117
Darwell's	Rev. J. Darwell	T. E. J.	15, 145, 300
Knaresborough (or Gopsal, or Handel's 148th)	G. F. Handel, 1742 (from the Fitzwilliam MS.) ..	Maurice (Choral Harmony) ..	237
Lawes's 148th	Henry Lawes, 1636 ..	Chiefly Maurice (Choral Harmony)	50
6 6, 8, 4.			
Leoni	Ancient Hebrew Melody ..	Maurice (Choral Harmony) ..	79
6 6, 4, 6 6 6, 4.			
*Fiat Lux	H. Handel Gear	H. Handel Gear..	60
6 5, 6 5, 6 5, 6 5.			
Bohemia	German	T. E. J.	99
Grosvenor	Dr. Steggall, 1853 ..	Maurice (Choral Harmony) ..	63
Labrador	Rev. C. Gregor's Collection ..	Maurice (Choral Harmony) ..	210
*St. Sylvester	Professor Oakeley ..	Professor Oakeley.. ..	27
6 4, 6 4, 6 6, 4.			
Scala Coeli (or St. Alphege)	W. H. Longhurst	W. H. Longhurst (Canterbury Psalmist)	326
5 5, 7 7 7 7, 6.			
*Chara	J. Hatherly, Mus. Bac. ..	J. Hatherley	159
IRREGULAR.			
*Chant	E. Hake, 1866	E. Hake	62
*Ezekiel	Henry Alford, 1866 ..	T. E. J.	213
*Misericordia	Henry Alford, 1866 ..	T. E. J.	191
Troyte	A. H. D. Troyte	A. H. D. Troyte	192

ALPHABETICAL INDEX OF TUNES.

N.B.—*Those marked with an asterisk * have been composed for, or first printed in, the present work.*

Name of Tune.	Measure.	Hymn.
Abbey	C.M.	161
All Saints (see Martyrdom)		
All Souls'	L.M.	93
Alnwick	6 6 6 6, 8 8	117
Alpha (see St. Alphege)		
Altona (or Breslau)	L.M.	120
Altorf (or Eisleben, or Luther's)	{ 8 7, 8 7, 8 8 7 ... ... { or 7 8s	13, 122 296
Angels'	6 8s	44, 140
Angelus	L.M.	314
Annue Christe	8 6s	129
Antioch	6 8s	219
Arundel	L.M.	231
Babylon Streams	L.M.	64, 241
Baden (or Nuremberg)	{ 8 8, 8 8 7 ... ... { or 8 7, 8 7, 4 4, 8 8	3, 303 209
Bamberg	L.M.	92
Basle (see Old 124th)		
Bavaria (or Potsdam)	L.M.	313
*Beaumont	4 6s	21, 126
Bedford	C.M.	23, 157, 222
Bedford (minor)	C.M.	83, 286
Benediction (see Salzburg)		
Ben Rhydding	S.M.	195
Bernard (see Hymn on Heaven)		
Bethlehem Ephratah (or Mendelssohn, or Praise)	10 7s	18
*Bochastle...	S.M.	227, 291
Bohemia	6 5, 6 5, 6 5, 6 5	99
Brasted	4 7s	256
Bremen (or Coburg)	8 7, 8 7	51, 235
Breslau (see Altona)		
Bristol	C.M.	279
Burford	C.M.	72, 285, 297
*Caen	7 5, 7 5...	257 (1)
Caithness	C.M.	289
Cannons...	L.M.	321
Capernaum (see Lustra Sex)		
Carisbrook	L.M.	199
Carlisle	C.M.	131
Caton (see Rockingham)		
Cassell (see also Werner)	8 7, 8 7, 7 7	167, 315
Ceylon	7 6, 7 6, 7 6, 7 6	42, 158, 266
*Chant	Irregular	62
Chapel Royal (see Hymnus Eucharisticus)		

Name of Tune.	Measure.	Hymn.
*Chara	5 5, 7 7 7, 6	159
Chestergate	8 8 8 6	183
Chichester (Old, or Exeter)	C.M.	189, 239
Chorale 37 (or Gotha, or St. Elizabeth)	L.M.	113
Chorale 82	L.M.	115, 151
Chorale 100 (see Magdeburg)		
Christmas Choral (see Eisleben)		
Coburg (see Bremen)		
Colchester	C.M.	177
Colmar	6 8s	192, 240
Constance	L.M.	198
Corinth (see Salzburg)		
Crasselius (or Winchester New)	L.M.	9, 258, 309
Crete	L.M.	272 (2)
Crüger	8 6, 8 6, 8 8	168
Culbach	8 7, 8 7	137
Culross	C.M.	73
Dantzick	7 7 7, 5	16, 88
Darwell's (or Olney)	6 6 6 6, 8 8	15, 145, 300
Delaware	{ 7 6, 7 6	105
	{ 4 7s	171
*Dies Iræ	9 7s	56, 57
Dix	4 7s	19, 153
Dorchester (or Stockport, or Yorkshire)	6 10s	17
Dort	S.M.	196, 251
Dortmund	L.M.	169
Dowland	8 7s	319
Dundee (see French and Windsor)		
Durham (see Innocents)		
Easter Hymn (see Worgan's)	... ...	
*Eastham	7 6, 7 6, 7 6, 7 6 ...	229, 294
Eatington	C.M.	234
Eaton	6 8s	201
Ein' feste Burg (or Fortress, or Worms) ...	8 7, 8 7, 6 6 6, 7 ...	228
Eisleben (or Christmas Choral, or Erfurt; see also } Altorf) ... ... }	L.M.	146, 248, 323
Ellesmere	L.M.	307
Ely (see Ten Commandments, or Sharon)		
Elvey (or St. George's)	8 7s	107, 225, 275
*Epiphany	6 7s and 4	32
Eppendorff	L.M.	139, 306
Erfurt (see Eisleben)		
Eucharistic Hymn (see Goudimel)		
Eventide	4 10s	318
Ewing (see Hymn on Heaven)		
Exeter (see Chichester)		
*Ezekiel	Irregular	213
Farrant (or Gloucester)	C.M.	324
*Fiat Lux	6 6 4, 6 6 6 4	60
Flanders (see Hamburgh)		

Name of Tune.	Measure.	Hymn.
Fortress (see Ein' feste Burg)		
Franconia	S.M.	6, 173
Frankfort	4 7s	95
French (or Dundee)	C.M.	114, 244
Freudenberg	L.M.	278
Gibbons (or Southminster, or Whitehall)	4 7s	2
Gibbons's St. Matthias	C.M.	53, 180
Gloucester (see also Farrant)	C.M.	86, 202
Goldbach	7 6, 7 6, 7 6, 7 6	58, 236
Gopsal (see Knaresborough)		
Gotha (see also Chorale 37)	8 7, 8 7	200
Göttingen	8 7, 8 7, 8 7	4
Goudimel (or Eucharistic Hymn, or Navarre) ...	9 8, 9 8, 9 8, 9 8	172
Gräfrath (or Ulm)	4 7s	38
Grosvenor	6 5, 6 5, 6 5, 6 5	63
Hackney (see St. Mary's)		
Hamburgh (or Flanders)	8 7s	49, 147
Handel's 148th (see Knaresborough)		
Hanover	10 10, 11 11	39
Harston (or Upminster)	L.M.	69
Hatherton	8 8 8, 6	87
Hayes's 127th	C.M.	20, 254
Henneberg	7 6, 7 6	271
Hereford	C.M.	47, 218
Hernlein	4 7s	29
Herrnhutt	8 8 6, 8 8 6	206
Holy Trinity	12, 12, 12, 10	144
Howard (or Lancaster, or St. Clement's)	C.M.	252
Hymn on Heaven (or Bernard, or Ewing, or St. Bede)	7 6, 7 6, 7 6, 7 6	128, 325
Hymnus Eucharisticus (or Chapel Royal, or Magdalene, or Magdalen College)	L.M.	89, 174
Innocents (or Durham, or Ratisbon)	4 7s	54, 226, 281, 301
Irons (or Southwell)	C.M.	112, 203
Jersey	4 7s	165
Kent	C.M.	247
*Kidbrook	7 7 7, 6	125 (2)
King's College (see Lawes's 148th)		
Knaresborough (or Gopsal, or Handel's 148th) ...	6 6 6 6, 8 8	237
Knecht (see Vienna)		
Labrador	6 5, 6 5, 6 5, 6 5	210
Lancaster (see Howard)		
Lawes (or Shropshire, or Whitehall)	4 7s	59, 264
Lawes's 148th (or King's College)	6 6 6 6, 8 8	50
Leipsic	L.M.	90, 149
Leoni	6 6, 8 4	79
London New (or Newtown)	C.M.	116, 249

Name of Tune.	Measure.	Hymn.
Paraclete...	7 7 7	124
Peterborough	C.M.	36, 224
Playford (or Salisbury)	L.M.	270
Potsdam (see also Bavaria)	8.M	207, 253
Prague (see also Praise and Tytherton)...	8 7, 8 7...	127
Praise (or Prague ; see also Bethlehem Ephratah)	7 6, 7 6, 7 6, 7 6	216
Prayer	L.M.	85
Presburg...	6 7s	100
Quam Dilecta	4 6s	170
*Quinquagesima	8 5, 8 5...	68
Ratisbon (see also Innocents)	6 7s	41, 148, 214, 310
*Redemption	4 7s	74
Reinagle (or St. Peter's, Oxford)	C.M.	187, 305
Reliance (see Tallis's Ordinal)		
Richmond	D.C.M.	78
Rockingham (or Caton)	L.M.	5, 104, 292
St. Albinus	7 8, 7 8, and Hallelujah	110, 111
St. Alphege (or Alpha ; see also Scala Cœli)	7 6, 7 6...	11
St. Ann's	C.M.	212, 282
St. Boniface (see Vienna)		
St. Bride	S.M.	184, 298
St. Clement (see also Howard)	L.M.	76
St. Columba	4 7s	22
St. David	C.M.	28, 194, 255
St. Elizabeth (see Chorale 37)		
*St. Gabriel	7 5, 7 5...	257 (2)
St. Gall	L.M.	118
St. George (see also Elvey)	C.M.	8, 135
St. James	C.M.	43, 150
St. Magnus (see Nottingham) ...		
St. Mark (see Ten Commandments)		
St. Mary's (or Hackney)	C.M.	31, 284
St. Matthew	D.C.M.	96, 283
St. Matthias (see also under Gibbons)	6 8s	182, 317
St. Michael's	S.M.	1, 230, 259
St. Mildred's	C.M.	260
St. Peter's (see also Reinagle)	S.M.	12, 204
St. Stephen's (or Nayland)	C.M.	181, 304
*St. Sylvester	6 5, 6 5, 6 5, 6 5	27
St. Theodulph (see Teschner)		
*St. Thomas	4 7s	71
St. Werburghs (see Salzburg)		
Salisbury (see also Playford)	C.M.	193
*Salve Caput	8 8 8 8, 7 (trochaic) ...	102
Salzburg (or Benediction, or Corinth, or St. Werbergh's, or Tantum Ergo) ... ... }	8 7, 8 7, 8 7	14
Savoy (or Old 100th)	L.M.	268, 287, 322
Saxony (see also Wise)	L.M.	94
Scala Cœli (or St. Alphege)	6 4, 6 4, 6 6 4	326
Seir	8 7s	265
Sephar	4 7s	290

Name of Tune.	Measure.	Hymn.
Sharon (see Elvey)...		
Shropshire (see Lawes)		
Southminster (see Gibbons)		
Southwell (see also Irons)	S.M.	10
Stockport (see Dorchester)		
*Starcross	8 8 8, 6, trochaic... ...	4
Stuttgart	8 7, 8 7, 8 7, 8 7	299
Sunday Tune	C.M.	121, 217
Supplication	S.M.	263
*Sursum Corda	4 6s	134
Swabia	S.M.	156
Tallis's Canon (or Magdalen)	L.M.	238, 312
Tallis's Ordinal (or Reliance, or Veni Creator) ...	C.M.	52, 274, 288
Tallis's Veni Creator	L.M.	138, 272 (1)
Tantum Ergo (see Salzburg)		
Ten Commandments (or Ely, or Magdeburg, or St. Mark) ... ... }	L.M.	136, 311
*Tenbury	7 75, 7 7 4	208
*Tenebræ	5 8s	101
Teschner (or Missionary Hymn, or St. Theodulph, or Waterford) ... ... }	7 6, 7 6, 7 6, 7 6	70, 132
Towy	7 7 7, 6	125 (1)
Tranby	8 7, 8 7	119, 243
Troyte	Irregular	162
Turnau	8 7, 8 7	221
Tytherton (or Moravia, or Prague)	S.M.	34, 164
Ulm (see Gräfrath)		
Upminster (see Harston)		
Upsal	8 4, 8 4, 8 8 8 4	316
Veni Creator (see Tallis's Ordinal)		
Vienna (or Knecht, or St. Boniface)	4 7s	37, 142
Vulpius (or Weimar)	8 7s	133, 179
Waldeck	L.M.	273, 308
Wareham	L.M.	40, 143, 269
*Warfare	8 7s	166
Waterford (see Teschner)		
Weimar (see also Vulpius)	L.M.	33, 320
Werner (or Cassell)	6 7s	67, 293
Wheatfield	8 7s	141, 276
Whitehall (see Gibbons and Lawes)		
Winchester, New (see Crasselius)		
Winchester, Old	C.M.	24, 154
Windsor (or Dundee)	C.M.	81, 190
Wise (or Saxony)	L.M.	302
Wittemberg (see Nun danket alle Gott)		
Worgan's (or Easter Hymn)	4 7s and Hallelujah ...	106
Worms (see Ein' feste Burg)		
York	C.M.	109
Yorkshire (see Dorchester)		

THE YEAR OF PRAISE

First Sunday in Advent.

ST. MICHAEL.

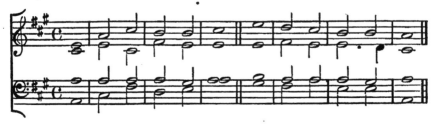

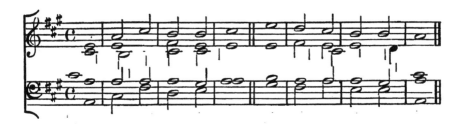

THE voice of one that cries
    Along the wilds untrod;
Prepare ye in the wilderness
    A highway for our God.

Be every valley raised,
    And every hill made low;
The crooked straight, the rugged plain;
    For God hath willed it so.

The glory of the Lord
    To all men shall appear;
His Word shall sound throughout the world,
    And every nation hear.

Man's glory is a flower,
    The flesh of man is grass:
Only the promise of our God
    Is now, and ever was.

First Sunday in Advent.

HARK, a glad exulting throng:
   Hark, the loud hosannas ring:
Glad hosannas loud and long
   Greet Messiah triumphing.

He, of whom the Prophets won
   Mystic visions faint and dim,
Comes, the Father's only Son,
   And Redemption comes with Him.

Lo, the Godhead come to earth,
   Perfect Man, as all might see,
That re-born in God's new birth
   Might the fallen manhood be.

So, when earth His terrors shake,
   He shall come our faith to bless:
Saved, for that first Advent's sake,
   By His glorious lowliness.

First Sunday in Advent.

Hymn 3.   III.   BADEN.

HOSANNA to the living Lord!
Hosanna to the Incarnate Word!
To Christ, Creator, Saviour, King,
Let earth, let heaven, hosanna sing!
Hosanna in the highest.

Hosanna, Lord, Thine angels cry:
Hosanna, Lord, Thy saints reply:
Above, beneath us, and around,
The dead and living swell the sound:
Hosanna in the highest.

O Saviour, with protecting care,
Be with us in Thy house of prayer,
Assembled in Thy sacred name,
While we Thy parting promise claim:
Hosanna in the highest.

But chiefest in our cleansed breast,
Eternal, bid Thy Spirit rest,
And make our secret soul to be
A temple pure, and worthy Thee:
Hosanna in the highest.

So in the last and dreadful day,
When earth and heaven shall melt away,
Thy flock, redeemed from sinful stain,
Shall swell the sound of praise again:
Hosanna in the highest.

First Sunday in Advent.

Hymn 4.　　　　　　　　　IV.　　　　　　　　GÖTTINGEN.

O'ER the distant mountains breaking,
  Comes the reddening dawn of day ;
Rise, my soul, from sleep awaking,
  Rise and sing, and watch and pray :
      'Tis thy Saviour,
  On His bright returning way.

O Thou long expected, weary
  Waits my anxious soul for Thee ;
Life is dark, and earth is dreary,
  Where Thy light I do not see :
      O my Saviour,
  When wilt Thou return to me ?

Long, too long in sin and sadness,
  Far away from Thee I pine,
When, O when, shall I the gladness
  Of Thy Spirit feel in mine ?
      O my Saviour,
  When shall I be wholly Thine ?

Nearer is my soul's salvation,
  Spent the night, the day at hand ;
Keep me in my lonely station,
  Watching for Thee till I stand,
      O my Saviour,
  In Thy bright and promised land.

With my lamp well trimmed and burning,
  Swift to hear, and slow to roam,
Watching for Thy glad returning,
  To restore me to my home :
      Come, my Saviour,
  O my Saviour, quickly come !

Hymn 5. L. ROCKINGHAM.

THAT day of wrath, that dreadful day,
  When heaven and earth shall pass away:
What power shall be the sinner's stay?
How shall he meet that dreadful day?

When, shrivelling like a parched scroll,
The flaming heavens together roll;
When louder yet, and yet more dread,
Swells the high trump that wakes the dead;

Oh, on that day, that wrathful day,
When man to judgment wakes from clay,
Be Thou the trembling sinner's stay,
Though heaven and earth shall pass away.

Hymn 6. II. FRANCONIA.

THE Son of Man shall come
With angel-hosts around,
'Mid darkening sun and falling stars,
And trumpet's solemn sound.

Awake, ye slumbering souls,
It is no time for rest:
He comes, as comes the lightning flash
Shining from east to west.

Thy servants, Lord, prepare
For that tremendous day:
Fill every heart with watchful care,
And stir us up to pray.

Help us to wait the hour
In toil and holy fear,
When, manifested with Thy saints,
Thou shalt again appear.

Then when the wailing earth
Thy sign in heaven shall see,
Thou shalt send forth Thine angel-band,
To gather us to Thee.

Second Sunday in Advent.

Hymn 7.   III.   OLD 34TH.

THE Church has waited long
   Her absent Lord to see :
And still in loneliness she waits,
   A friendless stranger she.
   Age after age has gone,
   Sun after sun has set,
And, still in weeds of widowhood,
   She weeps a mourner yet.

Saint after saint on earth
   Has lived, and loved, and died :
And as they left us one by one,
   We laid them side by side ;
   We laid them down to sleep,
   But not in hope forlorn :
We laid them but to ripen there,
   Till the last glorious morn.

The whole Creation groans,
   And waits to hear that voice,
That shall restore her comeliness,
   And make her wastes rejoice.
   Come, Lord, and wipe away
   The curse, the sin, the stain,
And make this blighted world of ours
   Thine own fair world again.

Second Sunday in Advent.

HARK the glad sound, the
    Saviour comes,
  The Saviour promised long,
Let every heart prepare a throne,
  And every voice a song.

He comes, the prisoners to release,
  In Satan's bondage held ;
The gates of brass before Him burst,
  The iron fetters yield.

He comes, the broken heart to bind,
  The bleeding soul to cure,
And with the riches of His grace
  To bless the humble poor.

Our glad hosannas, Prince of Peace,
  Thy welcome shall proclaim,
And heaven's eternal arches ring
  With Thy beloved name.

Third Sunday in Advent.

WHEN Christ the Lord would
    come on earth,
His messenger before Him went;
The greatest born of mortal birth,
    And charged with words of deep
      intent.

The least of all that here attend
    Hath honour greater far than he;
He was the Bridegroom's joyful friend,
    His Body and His Spouse are we.

A higher race, the sons of light,
    Of water and the Spirit born;
He, the last star of parting night,
    And we the children of the morn.

And as he boldly spake Thy Word,
    And joyed to hear the Bridegroom's
      voice;
Thus may Thy pastors teach, O Lord,
    And thus Thy hearing Church re-
      joice.

Third Sunday in Advent.

COME to Thy temple, Lord,
    Thy waiting Church to bless :
Let here Thy glory be adored,
    Give here Thy Word success.

Our inmost hearts refine,
    And for Thyself prepare :
Cast out all thoughts but thoughts divine,
    And reign triumphant there.

Thy servants, Lord, we are,
    Baptized into Thy name :
All hurtful things put from us far,
    All works of sin and shame.

Come to Thy temple, Lord,
    Thine own assembly bless :
That all may offer with accord
    Offerings of righteousness.

Third Sunday in Advent.

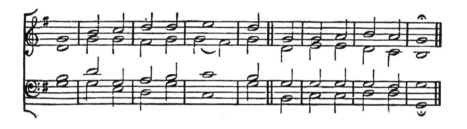

REJOICE, rejoice, believers,
   And let your lights appear;
The evening is advancing,
   The darker night is near.

The Bridegroom is arising,
   And soon He will draw nigh:
Up! watch, and pray, and wrestle,
   At midnight comes the cry.

See that your lamps are burning,
   Replenish them with oil,
Look now for your salvation,
   The end of sin and toil.

The watchers on the mountain
   Proclaim the Bridegroom near;
Go meet Him as He cometh,
   With Hallelujahs clear.

Our hope and expectation,
   O Jesu, now appear,
Arise, Thou Sun so looked for,
   O'er this benighted sphere:

With hands and hearts uplifted,
   We plead, O Lord, to see
The day of our redemption,
   And ever be with Thee.

Third Sunday in Advent.

COME, Kingdom of our God,
 Sweet reign of life and love,
Shed peace, and hope, and joy abroad,
 And wisdom from above.

Over our spirits first
 Extend thy healing reign ;
Then raise and quench the sacred thirst
 That never pains again.

Come, Kingdom of our God,
 And make the broad earth thine,
Stretch o'er her land and isles the rod
 That flowers with grace divine.

Soon may all tribes be blest
 With fruit from Life's glad tree :
And in its shade like brothers rest,
 Sons of one family.

Come, Kingdom of our God,
 And raise thy glorious throne
In worlds by the undying trod,
 When God shall bless His own.

Fourth Sunday in Advent.

G REAT God, what do I see and hear?
 The end of things created :
The Judge of mankind does appear,
 On clouds of glory seated ;
The trumpet sounds, the graves restore
The dead which they contained before :
 Prepare, my soul, to meet Him.

Fourth Sunday in Advent.

Hymn 14.   II.   SALZBURG.

Major, for verses 1, 3, 4.

Minor, for verse 2.

L O! He comes, with clouds descending,
        Once for favoured sinners slain ;
Thousand thousand saints attending,
        Swell the triumph of His train :
                Hallelujah !
        God appears on earth to reign !

Every eye shall now behold Him
        Robed in dreadful majesty ;
Those who set at nought and sold Him,
        Pierced and nailed Him to the tree,
                Deeply wailing,
        Shall the true Messiah see.

Now Redemption, long expected,
        See in solemn pomp appear !
All His saints, by man neglected,
        Now shall meet Him in the air :
                Hallelujah !
        See the day of God appear !

Yea, Amen ! let all adore Thee,
        High on Thine eternal throne ;
Saviour, take the power and glory ;
        Claim the kingdom for Thine own :
                O come quickly,
        Everlasting God, come down !

Fourth Sunday in Advent.

R EJOICE, the Lord is King,
  Your Lord and King adore:
Mortals, give thanks and sing,
And triumph evermore:
Lift up your heart, lift up your voice,
Rejoice, again I say, rejoice.

Jesus the Saviour reigns,
  The God of truth and love:
When He had purged our stains,
  He took His seat above:
Lift up your heart, lift up your voice,
Rejoice, again I say, rejoice.

He sits at God's right hand
  Till all His foes submit,
And bow to His command,
  And fall beneath His feet:
Lift up your heart, lift up your voice,
Rejoice, again I say, rejoice.

Rejoice in glorious hope:
  Jesus the Judge shall come
And take His servants up
  To their eternal home:
We soon shall hear th' Archangel's voice,
The trump of God shall sound, rejoice.

Fourth Sunday in Advent.

Hymn 16.   IV.   DANTZICK.

Major, for verses 1, 4.

Minor, for verses 2, 3.

COME, Lord Jesus, quickly come:
　Lo, Thy Church with longing eye,
Lifts her blended voices high,
　　Not a lip is dumb.

They who now with many a tear,
In the dry and stubborn soil,
Mourning, ask from out their toil,
　　" Master, art Thou near ? "

Watchers of the weary night,
While they pace their lonely round,
Listen for the trumpet's sound,
　　Seek the dawning light.

When shall lighten forth Thy sign
Through the heavens ? O Lord, how long ?
When, amid the radiant throng,
　　Shall Thy coming shine ?

Christmas Day.

DORCHESTER.

CHRISTIANS, awake; salute the happy morn
    Whereon the Saviour of mankind was born;
Rise to adore the mystery of love,
Which hosts of angels chanted from above:
With them the joyful tidings first begun,
Of God Incarnate and the Virgin's Son.

Then to the watchful shepherds it was told,
Who heard th' angelic herald's voice, " Behold,
I bring glad tidings of a Saviour's birth
To you and all the nations upon earth:
This day hath God fullfilled His promised word,
This day is born a Saviour, Christ the Lord."

Artless and watchful as these favoured swains,
While virgin meekness in the heart remains,
Trace we the Babe who has retrieved our loss,
From His poor manger to His bitter cross:
Tread in His steps, assisted by His grace,
Till man's first heavenly state again takes place.

Then may we hope, th' angelic thrones among,
To sing in heaven a glad triumphant song;
He that was born upon this joyful day
Around us all His glory shall display:
Saved by His love, for ever we shall sing
Glory to God on high, our heavenly King.

Christmas Day.

II. BETHLEHEM EPHRATAH.

HARK! the herald angels sing
    Glory to the new-born King,
Peace on earth and mercy mild,
God and sinners reconciled.
Joyful all ye nations rise,
Join the triumph of the skies;
With the angelic host proclaim,
Christ is born in Bethlehem.
   Hark! the herald angels sing
   Glory to the new-born King.

Christ, by highest heaven adored,
Christ the Everlasting Lord,
Late in time behold Him come,
Offspring of a virgin's womb.
Veiled in flesh the Godhead see:
Hail, the Incarnate Deity!
Pleased as man with men to dwell,
Jesus, our Emmanuel.
   Hark! the herald angels sing
   Glory to the new-born King.

Hail, the heaven born Prince of Peace!
Hail, the Sun of Righteousness!
Light and life to all He brings,
Risen with healing on His wings,
Mild He lays His glory by,
Born that man no more may die:
Born to raise the sons of earth,
Born to give them second birth.
   Hark! the herald angels sing
   Glory to the new-born King.

Christmas Day.

B RIGHT and joyful is the morn,
    For to us a Child is born ;
From the highest realms of heaven
Unto us a Son is given.

On His shoulder He shall bear
Power and majesty, and wear
On His vesture and His thigh,
Names most awful, names most high.

Wonderful in counsel He,
The Incarnate Deity :
Sire of ages ne'er to cease,
King of Kings, and Prince of Peace.

Come and worship at His feet,
Yield to Christ the homage meet,
From His manger to His throne,—
Homage due to God alone.

Christmas Day.

WHILE shepherds watched their
    flocks by night,
All seated on the ground,
The angel of the Lord came down,
    And glory shone around.

Fear not, said he, for mighty dread
    Had seized their troubled mind,
Glad tidings of great joy I bring
    To you and all mankind.

To you in David's town this day
    Is born of David's line,
A Saviour, who is Christ the Lord,—
    And this shall be *the* *sign :*

The heavenly Babe you there shall find
    To human view displayed,
All meanly wrapt in swathing-bands,
    And in a manger laid.

Thus spake the seraph, and forthwith
    Appeared a shining throng
Of angels, praising God, and thus
    Addrest their joyful song :

All glory be to God on high,
    And to the earth be peace :
Good-will henceforth from heaven to
    men
    Begin, and never cease.

St. Stephen's Day.

BEAUMONT.

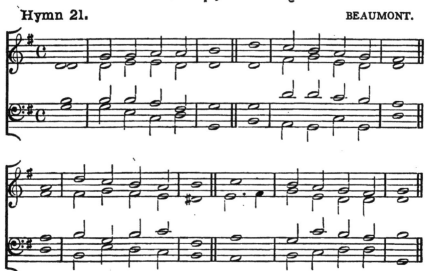

THE first who dared to die
    Had blessed visions given :
The glory on him shone
    Down from the open heaven.

Look up into the skies,
    Ye of the latter day :
The shining of that light
    Shall never pass away.

Your bitter foes in vain
    Their storms of malice shower :
Behold your Captain stand
    At God's right hand in power.

Each scattering of the Church
    The Word of God shall sow :
For every cruel stroke,
    The holy plant shall grow.

Lift up the voice of prayer
    Before your enemies ;
And from their very ranks
    Fresh martyrs shall arise.

St. John's Day.

ST. COLUMBA.

"LITTLE children, dwell in love
New begotten from above,
Ye by this your birth may know,
That ye dwell in love below.

" God your Father reigns on high,
Unbeheld by mortal eye ;
Him ye see not ; love Him then
In His types, your fellow-men.

" Not in semblance nor in word,
But in holy thoughts unheard,
But in very truth and deed,
Share their joy, and help their need."

Thus the saint whom Jesus loved
Spoke in word, in action proved :
Lord, may Thy disciples be
Like to Him, and like to Thee.

The Innocents' Day.

BEDFORD.

THE Lord our God is full of might,
   And reigns in highest bliss ;
All wisdom, power, and majesty
   For evermore are His.

He needeth not the strength of man
   To stand upon His side ;
Out of the mouths of sucking babes
   His name is glorified.

The race is not unto the swift,
   Nor to the strong the prize :
An infant band for Christ hath died,
   And enters first the skies.

Thus every station, every age,
   The creatures of His will,
His high behests of Providence
   In life and death fulfil.

Full many a soul by God held dear
   Man's pride hath overpast :
For there are last that shall be first,
   And first that shall be last.

Sunday after Christmas.

WINCHESTER.

THE race that long in darkness pined
   Have seen a glorious Light;
The people dwell in day who dwelt
   In Death's surrounding night.

To us a Child of Hope is born,
   To us a Son is given;
Him shall the tribes of earth obey,
   Him all the hosts of heaven.

His name shall be the Prince of Peace,
   For evermore adored;
The Wonderful, the Counsellor,
   The great and mighty Lord.

His power increasing still shall spread,
   His reign no end shall know;
Justice shall guard His throne above,
   And peace abound below.

Sunday after Christmas.

II. LUXEMBURG.

WHILE with ceaseless course the sun
    Hasted through the former year,
Many souls their race have run,
    Never more to meet us here.

Fixed in an eternal state,
    They have done with all below ;
We a little longer wait,
    But how little none can know.

Swiftly then our fleeting days
    Bear us down life's rapid stream ;
Lord, to heaven our wishes raise,
    All on earth is but a dream.

Bless Thy Word to young and old,
    Fill us with the Saviour's love ;
And, when life's short tale is told,
    May we dwell with Thee above.

Sunday after Christmas.

COME, Lord Jesus, take Thy rest
  In the convert sinner's breast;
Make the quickened heart Thy throne,
Son of God, the Virgin's Son.

God in man, Incarnate God,
Sinless Child of flesh and blood,
Man in God, Thy brethren we,
Raise us up to God in Thee.

Come and give us peace within,
Loose us from the bonds of sin,
Take away the galling weight
Laid on us by Satan's hate.

Give us grace Thy yoke to wear,
Give us strength Thy cross to bear;
Make us Thine in deed and word,
Thine in heart and life, O Lord.

Kill in us the carnal root,
That the Spirit may bear fruit;
Plant in us Thy holy mind,
Keep us faithful, loving, kind.

So, when Thou shalt come again,
Judge of angels and of men,
We with all Thy saints shall sing
Hallelujahs to our King.

Sunday after Christmas.

Hymn 27.   IV.   ST. SYLVESTER.

Minor, for verses 1 and 3.

Org. Ped. *senza Manuale.*

Col Manuale.

Major, for verses 2 and 4.

* *The small notes are not to be sung, they are for the Organ only.*

SET thine house in order,
  Thou shalt die, not live ;
May the voice to each one
  Solemn warning give :
Pilgrims here and strangers,
  Weak and frail alike,
·Who can tell among us
  Where the blow may strike ?

Set thine house in order,
  All its bulwarks tell ;
Try the ground beneath thee,
  Stir and delve it well :
Soon shall break the tempest;
  Wouldst thou bide the shock ?
Hearer be and doer,
  Founded on the rock.

Set thine house in order,
  Search and·sweep it clean,
That God's Spirit loathe not
  To abide therein.
Thoughts and plans unholy,
  Schemes that shun the day ;
Pride, and greed, and rancour,
  Purge them all away.

Set thine house in order,
  Gather up thy stores,
Every weapon brighten
  For thy Captain's wars :
Sort out all thy treasures,
  Earthly dross remove ;
Three alone are lasting,
  Faith, and Hope, and Love.

The Circumcision of Christ.

THY blood, O Christ, hath made our peace :
    Not only that, whereby
The ground of Calvary was stained,
    When Thou wert hung on high ;

Nor only that, which in Thine hour
    Of fear and agony,
Distilled upon Thy trembling frame
    In dark Gethsemane :

But that shed from Thee, when at first
    In childhood Thou didst deign
Thus to endure for sinful man
    The legal rite of pain.

And as with suffering and with Thee
    Our yearly course begins ;
So teach us to renounce the flesh
    And put away our sins ;

That in the Israel of Thy Church
    We may not lose our part :
In spirit and in body pure,
    And circumcised in heart.

The Circumcision of Christ.

JESUS! Name of priceless worth,
 To the fallen sons of earth,
For the promise that it gave,
"Jesus shall His people save."

Jesus! Name of mercy mild,
Given to the Holy Child,
When the cup of human woe
First He tasted here below.

Jesus! Only name that's given
Under all the mighty heaven,
Whereby man, to sin enslaved,
Bursts his fetters, and is saved.

Jesus! Name of wondrous love!
Human name of Him above:
Pleading only this we flee,
Helpless, O *our* God, to Thee.

The Circumcision of Christ.

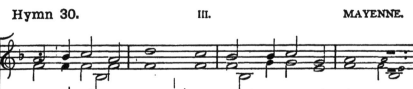

FOR Thy mercy and Thy grace,
   Faithful through another year,
Hear our song of thankfulness,
   Father and Redeemer, hear !
In our weakness and distress,
   Rock of Strength, be Thou our stay :
In the pathless wilderness
   Be our true and living way.

Who of us death's awful road
   In the coming year shall tread ?
With Thy rod and staff, O God,
   Comfort Thou his dying head.
Keep us faithful, keep us pure,
   Keep us evermore Thine own :
Help, O help us to endure :
   Fit us for the promised crown.

The Circumcision of Christ.

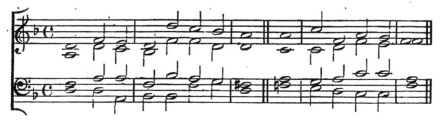

O GOD, our help in ages past,
  Our hope for years to come,
Our shelter from the stormy blast,
  And our eternal home :

Before the hills in order stood,
  Or earth received her frame,
From everlasting Thou art God,
  To endless years the same.

A thousand ages in Thy sight
  Are like an evening gone ;
Short as the watch that ends the night,
  Before the rising sun.

Time, like an ever-rolling stream,
  Bears all its sons away ;
They fly forgotten, as a dream
  Dies at the opening day.

O God, our help in ages past,
  Our hope for years to come,
Be Thou our guard while troubles last,
  And our eternal home.

The Epiphany.

EPIPHANY.

Hail, hail, Lord Je - - - sus.

THOU that art the Father's Word,
     Thou that art the Lamb of God,
Thou that art the Virgin's Son,
Thou that savest souls undone,
Sacred sacrifice for sin,
Fount of piety within,
          Hail, Lord Jesus.

Thou to whom Thine angels raise
Quiring songs of sweetest praise,
Thou that art the flower and fruit,
Virgin-born from Jesse's root,
Shedding holy peace abroad,
Perfect man and perfect God,
          Hail, Lord Jesus.

Thou that art the door of heaven,
Living bread in mercy given,
Brightness of the Father's face,
Everlasting Prince of Peace,
Precious pearl beyond all price,
Brightest star in all the skies,
          Hail, Lord Jesus.

King and spouse of holy hearts,
Fount of love that ne'er departs,
Sweetest life, and brightest day,
Truest truth, and surest way
That leads onward to the blest
Sabbath of eternal rest,
          Hail, Lord Jesus.

The Epiphany.

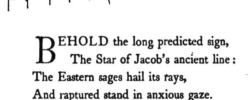

B EHOLD the long predicted sign,
  The Star of Jacob's ancient line:
The Eastern sages hail its rays,
And raptured stand in anxious gaze.

And soon within their hearts there shine
Rays fairer still and more divine,
Which gently summon them to rise
And trust the guidance of the skies.

When God commands, the wise obey:
Love sees no danger in the way:
House, neighbours, friends, their steps recall;
The voice of God outweighs them all.

O while the star of heavenly grace
Invites us, Lord, to seek Thy face,
May we no more that grace repel,
Nor quench that light which shines so well.

The Epiphany.

O LORD our God, arise,
   The cause of truth maintain ;
And wide o'er all the peopled world
   Extend her blessed reign.

Thou Prince of Life, arise,
   Nor let Thy conquests cease :
Far spread the glory of Thy name,
   And bless the earth with peace.

Thou Holy Ghost, arise,
   Expand Thy quickening wing ;
And o'er a dark and ruined world
   Let light and order spring.

All on the earth, arise,
   To God the Saviour sing :
From shore to shore, from earth to heaven,
   Let the loud anthem ring.

The Epiphany.

Hymn 35.   IV.   NASSAU.

A S with gladness men of old
    Did the guiding star behold :
As with joy they hailed its light,
Leading onward, beaming bright :
So, most gracious Lord, may we
Evermore be led to Thee.

As with joyful steps they sped
To that lowly manger-bed,
There to bend the knee before
Him whom heaven and earth adore .
So may we with willing feet
Ever seek the mercy-seat.

As they offered gifts most rare
At that manger rude and bare :
So may we with holy joy,
Pure and free from sin's alloy,
All our costliest treasures bring,
Christ, to Thee, our heavenly King.

Holy Jesus, every day
Keep us in the narrow way ;
And, when earthly things are past,
Bring our ransomed souls at last
Where they need no star to guide,
Where no clouds Thy glory hide.

In the heavenly country bright
Need they no created light :
Thou its light, its joy, its crown,
Thou its sun which goes not down :
There for ever may we sing
Hallelujahs to our King.

First Sunday after Epiphany.

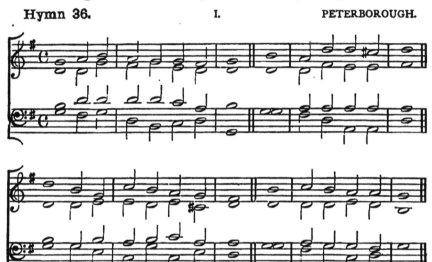

A S to His earthly parents' home
    Went down the Holy Child,
And found His Father's business there,
    Subjection meek and mild :

And as obedience all those years
    In lowly Nazareth
Forsook Him not, but bore Him on,
    Obedient unto death :

So by Thy mercies teach us, Lord,
    Our sacrifice to bring,
Our treasures, heart, and life, and love,
    To spread before our King.

Thy presence is our guiding star,
    We seek Thy holy hill :
Transform us, Lord, renew our minds,
    To prove Thy perfect will.

First Sunday after Epiphany.

Hymn 37.   II.   VIENNA.

SONS of men, behold from far,
　　Hail the long-expected star;
Jacob's star that gilds the night,
Guides bewildered nature right.

Mild it shines on all beneath,
Piercing through the shades of death,
Scattering error's wide-spread night,
Kindling darkness into light.

Nations all, remote and near,
Haste to see your God appear;
Haste, for Him your hearts prepare,
Meet Him manifested there.

There behold the day-spring rise,
Pouring light upon your eyes:
See it chase the shades away,
Shining unto perfect day.

Sing, ye morning stars, again,
God descends on earth to reign;
Deigns for man His life to employ;
Shout, ye sons of God, for joy.

Hymn 38.   III.   GRÄFRATH.

TO Thy temple we repair :
  Lord, we love to worship there :
When within the veil we meet
Christ before the mercy-seat.

While Thy glorious praise is sung,
Touch our lips, unloose our tongue,
That our joyful souls may bless   .
Thee the Lord our Righteousness.

While the prayers of saints ascend,
God of love, to ours attend :
Hear us, for Thy Spirit pleads :
Hear, for Jesus intercedes.

While Thy ministers proclaim
Peace and pardon in Thy name,
Through their voice by faith may we
Hear the Word of power from Thee.

From Thy house when we return,
May our hearts within us burn :
And at evening let us say,
We have walked with God to day !.

Hymn 39.　　　　　　IV.　　　　　　HANOVER.

Y E servants of God,
　Your Master proclaim ;
And publish abroad
　His wonderful name ;
The name all victorious
　Of Jesus extol;
His kingdom is glorious,
　And rules over all.

God ruleth on high,
　Almighty to save ;
And still He is nigh,
　His presence we have :

The great congregation
　His triumph shall sing,
Ascribing salvation
　To Jesus our King.

Then let us adore,
　And give Him His right ;
All glory and power,
　And wisdom and might ;
All honour and blessing,
　With angels above ;
And thanks never ceasing,
　And infinite love.

Second Sunday after Epiphany.

Hymn 40.　　　　　　　I.　　　　　　　WAREHAM.

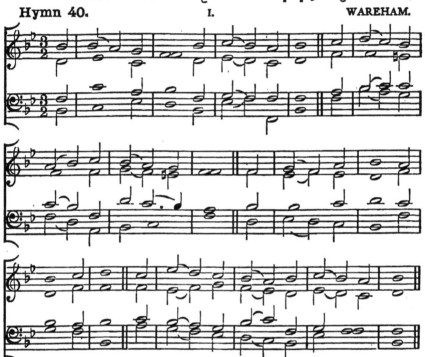

THROUGH Israel's coasts, in times of old,
　When Thou didst dwell with men below,
By signs and wonders manifold
　Thou didst, O Lord, Thy glory shew.

But not alone Thy mighty power
　Shone forth from every wondrous sign:
Day unto day, and hour to hour,
　Spoke forth Thy love and grace divine.

And now Thou reignest, Lord, above,
　We none the less Thy wonders trace:
Unwearied are Thy calls of love,
　Unspent Thy miracles of grace.

Thou who didst make the water wine,
　Our earthly with Thy heavenly fill:
Our scant obedience change to Thine,
　Our passions to Thy blessed will.

Hymn 41.   II.   RATISBON.

JESUS, God of love, attend,
  From Thy glorious throne descend;
Set, O set the captives free,
Draw our backward souls to Thee :
Let us all from Thee receive
Light to see, and life to live.

Let us hear Thy pardoning voice
Bid the contrite heart rejoice :
Prayer can mercy's door unlock,
Open, Lord, to us that knock :
Us the heirs of glory seal,
With Thy benediction fill.

Give the heavy-laden rest,
Shed Thy love in every breast :
Witness all our sins forgiven :
Grant on earth a glimpse of heaven :
Bring the joyful tidings down,
Fit us for our future crown.

Second Sunday after Epiphany.

Hymn 42.   III.   CEYLON.

HAIL to the Lord's Anointed,
  Great David's greater Son!
Hail, in the time appointed,
  His reign on earth begun!
He comes, to break oppression,
  To set the captive free,
To take away transgression,
  And rule in equity.

He comes with succour speedy,
  To those who suffer wrong:
To help the poor and needy,
  And bid the weak be strong:
To give them songs for sighing,
  Their darkness turn to light,
Whose souls, condemned and dying,
  Were precious in His sight.

He shall come down like showers
  Upon the fruitful earth,
And love, joy, hope, like flowers,
  Spring in His path to birth:
Before Him on the mountains
  Shall Peace, the herald, go,
And righteousness in fountains
  From hill to valley flow.

Kings shall fall down before Him,
  And gold and incense bring:
All nations shall adore Him,
  His praise all people sing:
For He shall have dominion
  O'er river, sea, and shore,
Far as the eagle's pinion,
  Or dove's light wing can soar.

O'er every foe victorious
  He on His throne shall rest,
From age to age more glorious,
  All-blessing, and all-blest:
The tide of time shall never
  His covenant remove:
His name shall stand for ever,
  That name to us is Love.

Hymn 43.   IV.   ST. JAMES.

THE silent joy, that sinks so deep,
   Of confidence and rest,
Lulled in a father's arm to sleep,
   Or on a mother's breast:
Who but a Christian through all life
   That blessing may prolong?
Who through the world's sad day of strife
   Still chant his morning song?

Fathers may hate us or forsake,
   God's foundlings then are we:
Mother or child no pity take,
   But we shall still have Thee.
We may look home, and seek in vain
   A fond fraternal heart,
But Christ hath given His promise plain
   To act a brother's part.

Nor shall dull age, as worldlings say,
   The heavenward flame annoy:
The Saviour cannot pass away,
   And with Him lives our joy.
Such is Thy banquet, dearest Lord:
   O give us grace, to cast
Our lot with Thine, to trust Thy Word,
   And keep our best till last.

Third Sunday after Epiphany.

Hymn 44.   I.   ANGELS' SONG.

FORTH from the dark and stormy sky,
    Lord, to Thy altar's shade we fly;
Forth from the world, its hope and fear,
Saviour, we seek Thy shelter here:
Weary and weak, Thy grace we pray;
Turn not, O Lord, Thy guests away.

Long have we roamed in want and pain;
Long have we sought Thy rest in vain;
Wildered in doubt, in darkness lost,
Long have our souls been tempest-tost:
Low at Thy feet our sins we lay;
Turn not, O Lord, Thy guests away.

Third Sunday after Epiphany.

Hymn 45.　　　　　　　　　II.　　　　　　　MELCOMBE.

GOD, in the Gospel of His Son,
　Makes His eternal counsels known;
Where love in all its glory shines,
And truth is drawn in fairest lines.

The prisoner here may break his chains;
The weary rest from all his pains;
The captive feel his bondage cease;
The mourner find the way of peace.

Here faith reveals to mortal eyes
A brighter world beyond the skies;
Here shines the light which guides our way
From earth to realms of endless day.

Oh, grant us grace, Almighty Lord,
To mark and learn Thy holy Word;
Its truths with meekness to receive,
And by its holy precepts live.

Hymn 46. III. MAGL

HAIL the day when in the sky
　　Shone the day-spring from on high :
When the star from heaven displayed
Where the Holy Child was laid.

Onward moving that bright flame
Did the Saviour's birth proclaim :
And the Gentiles came to bring
Offerings to their Infant King.

Lord of Glory, may Thy light
Shine upon our darkened sight,
Till it guide us to the rest
Where Thy people shall be blest.

May it light us on the road,
Leading to the throne of God :
And our offering then shall be
Hearts devoted, Lord, to Thee.

Hymns of glory and of praise,
Father, unto Thee we raise :
Praise to Thee, O Christ our King,
And the Holy Ghost, we sing.

Third Sunday after Epiphany.

O THOU who hast Thy servants taught
   That not by words alone,
But by the fruits of holiness
   The life of God is shewn;

While in Thy house of prayer we meet,
   And call Thee God and Lord;
Give us an heart to follow Thee,
   Obedient to Thy Word.

When we our voices lift in praise,
   Give Thou us grace to bring
An offering of unfeigned thanks,
   And with the Spirit sing.

And in the dangerous path of life
   Uphold us as we go:
That with our lips and in our lives
   Thy glory we may shew.

Hymn 48. L. STARCROSS.

L O, the storms of life are breaking,—
  Faithless fears our hearts are shaking;
For our succour undertaking,
    Lord and Saviour, help us!

Lo, the world, from Thee rebelling,
Round Thy Church in pride is swelling:
With Thy Word their madness quelling,
    Lord and Saviour, help us!

On Thine own command relying,
We our onward task are plying;
Unto Thee for safety sighing,
    Lord and Saviour, help us!

By Thy birth, Thy cross, and passion,
By Thy tears of deep compassion,
By Thy mighty intercession,
    Lord and Saviour, help us!

Fourth Sunday after Epiphany.

Hymn 49. II. HAMBURGH.

JESU, lover of my soul,
  Let me to Thy bosom fly,
While the nearer waters roll,
  While the tempest still is nigh :
Hide me, O my Saviour, hide,
  Till the storm of life is past ;
Safe into the haven guide,
  O receive my soul at last.

Other refuge have I none ;
  Hangs my helpless soul on Thee :
Leave, ah leave me not alone,
  Still support and comfort me :
All my trust on Thee is stayed ;
  All my help from Thee I bring ;
Cover my defenceless head
  With the shadow of Thy wing.

Thou, O Christ, art all I want,
  More than all in Thee I find :
Raise the fallen, cheer the faint,
  Heal the sick, and lead the blind.
Just and holy is Thy name ;
  I am all unrighteousness : ·
Vile and full of sin I am ;
  Thou art full of truth and grace.

Plenteous grace with Thee is found,
  Grace to cover all my sin ;
Let the healing streams abound ;
  Make and keep me pure within :
Thou of life the fountain art,
  Freely let me take of Thee ;
Spring Thou up within my heart,
  Rise to all eternity.

Fourth Sunday after Epiphany.

Hymn 50.   III.   LAWES' 148TH

LORD of the worlds above,
  How pleasant and how fair
The dwellings of Thy love,
  Thy earthly temples are !
    To Thine abode
    My heart aspires,
    With warm desires
    To see my God.

O happy souls that pray
  Where God appoints to hear !
O happy men that pay
  Their constant service there !
    They praise Thee still ;
    And happy they
    That love the way
    To Sion's hill.

They go from strength to strength,
  Through this dark vale of tears,
Till each arrives at length,
  Till each in heaven appears :
    O glorious seat,
    When God our King
    Shall thither bring
    Our willing feet !

Hymn 51.   IV.   BREMEN.

A LL unseen the Master walketh
By the toiling servant's side :
Comfortable words He speaketh,
While His hands uphold and guide.

Grief, nor pain, nor any sorrow
Rends Thy heart, to Him unknown :
He to-day, and He to-morrow,
Grace sufficient gives His own.

Holy strivings nerve and strengthen,
Long endurance wins the crown :
When the evening shadows lengthen,
Thou shalt lay Thy burden down.

Hymn 52.   i.   TALLIS'S ORDINAL.

THE Angel comes, he comes to reap
   The harvest of the Lord:
O'er all the earth with fatal sweep
   Wide waves his flamy sword.

And who are they, in sheaves to bide
   The fire of vengeance bound?
The tares, whose rank luxuriant pride
   Choked the fair crop around.

And who are they, reserved in store,
   God's treasure-house to fill?
The wheat, a hundred-fold that bore
   Amid surrounding ill.

O King of Mercy, grant us power,
   Thy fiery wrath to flee:
In Thy destroying Angel's hour,
   O gather us to Thee.

Fifth Sunday after Epiphany.

Hymn 53.   II.   GIBBONS'S ST. MATTHIAS.

O UR God is love : and all His saints
     His image bear below ;
The heart, with love to God inspired,
     With love to man will glow.

O may we love each other, Lord,
     As we are loved of Thee :
For none are truly born of God
     Who live in enmity.

Heirs of the same immortal bliss,
     Our hopes and fears the same,
The cords of love our hearts should bind,
     The law of love inflame.

So shall the vain contentious world
     Our peaceful lives approve,
And wondering say, as they of old,
     " See how these Christians love."

Hymn 54.　　　　　　III.　　　　　　　INNOCENTS.

S ONGS of praise the angels sung,
　Heaven with Hallelujahs rung,
When Jehovah's work begun,
When He spake and it was done.

Songs of praise awoke the morn,
When the Prince of Peace was born:
Songs of praise arose, when He
Captive led captivity.

Heaven and earth must pass away,
Songs of praise shall crown that day:
God will make new heavens and earth,
Songs of praise shall hail their birth.

And shall man alone be dumb,
Till that glorious kingdom come?
No: the Church delights to raise
Psalms, and hymns, and songs of praise.

Saints below, with heart and voice,
Still in songs of praise rejoice:
Learning here, by faith and love,
Songs of praise to sing above.

Borne upon their latest breath,
Songs of praise shall conquer death:
Then, amidst eternal joy,
Songs of praise their powers employ.

Fifth Sunday after Epiphany.

O LORD, my best desire fulfil,
　　And help me to resign
Life, health, and comfort to Thy will,
　　And make Thy pleasure mine.

Why should I shrink at Thy command,
　　Whose love forbids my fears,
Or tremble at the gracious Hand
　　That wipes away my tears?

No, rather let me freely yield
　　What most I prize to Thee,
Who never hast a good withheld,
　　Or wilt withhold, from me.

Thy favour, all my journey through,
　　Thou art engaged to grant:
What else I want, or think I do,
　　'Tis better still to want.

Sixth Sunday after Epiphany.

Hymns 56, 57.   I., II.   DIES IRÆ.

DAY of anger, that dread day
　　Shall the sign in Heaven display,
And the earth in ashes lay.
O what trembling shall appear
When His coming shall be near,
Who shall all things strictly clear :
When the trumpet shall command,
Through the tombs of every land,
All before the throne to stand.

Death shall shrink and nature quake
When all creatures shall awake,
Answer to their Judge to make.
See the book divinely penned,
In which all is found contained,
Whence the world shall be arraigned.
When the Judge is on His throne,
All that's hidden shall be shewn,
Nought unpunished or unknown.

What shall I before Him say ?
How shall I be safe that day,
When the righteous scarcely may ?
King of awful majesty,
Saving sinners graciously,
Fount of mercy, save Thou me.
Leave me not, my Saviour; one
For whose soul Thy course was run,
Lest I be that day undone.

THOU didst toil my soul to gain,
　　Didst redeem me with Thy pain,
Be such labour not in vain.
Thou just Judge of wrath severe,
Grant my sins remission here,
Ere Thy reckoning day appear.
My transgressions grievous are,
Scarce look up for shame I dare :
Lord, thy guilty suppliant spare.

Thou didst heal the sinner's grief,
And didst hear the dying thief:
Even I may hope relief.
All unworthy is my prayer';
Make my soul Thy mercy's care,
And from fire eternal spare.
Place me with Thy sheep—that band
Who shall separated stand
From the goats, on Thy right hand.

When Thy voice in wrath shall say,
Cursed ones, depart away ;
Call me with the blest, I pray.
Lord, Thine ear in mercy bow ;
Broken is my heart and low :
Guard of my last end be Thou.
In that day, that mournful day,
When to judgment wakes our clay,
Shew me mercy, Lord, I pray.

Sixth Sunday after Epiphany.

Hymn 58.   III.   GOLDBACH.

JESUS, Thy love unbounded,
 So full, so sweet, so free,
Leaves all our thoughts confounded,
 Whene'er we think of Thee.
For us Thou cam'st from heaven,
 For us didst bleed and die,
That, ransomed and forgiven,
 We might ascend on high.

We know that Thou hast bought us,
 And washed us in Thy blood :
We know Thy grace has brought us
 As kings and priests to God.
We know that soon the morning,
 Long looked-for, hasteth near,
When we, at Thy returning,
 In glory shall appear.

O let Thy love constrain us
 To give our hearts to Thee :
Let nothing please or pain us,
 Apart, O Lord, from Thee :
Our joy, our one endeavour,
 Through suffering, conflict, shame,
To serve Thee, gracious Saviour,
 And magnify Thy name.

Hymn 59.   **IV.**   LAWES.

E ARTH is past away and gone,
All her glories every one :
All her pomp is broken down,
God is reigning—God alone !

All her high ones lowly lie,
All her mirth hath passed by,
All her merry-hearted sigh :
God is reigning—God on high !

No more sorrow, no more night ;
Perfect joy, and purest light ;
With His spotless saints and bright,
God is reigning in the height !

Blessing, praise, and glory bring ;
Offer every holy thing :
Everlasting praises sing ;
God is reigning, God our King !

Septuagesima Sunday.

Hymn 60. L. FIAT LUX.

Let there be light, Let there be light!

THOU, whose almighty word
Chaos and darkness heard,
And took their flight,
Hear us, we humbly pray,
And where the Gospel-day
Sheds not its glorious ray,
Let there be light!

Thou, who didst come to bring
On Thy redeeming wing
Healing and light,
Health to the sick in mind,
Sight to the inly blind,
O now to all mankind
Let there be light!

Spirit of truth and love,
Life-giving, holy Dove,
Speed forth Thy flight!
Move on the waters' face,
Bearing the lamp of grace,
And in earth's darkest place
Let there be light!

Blessed and holy Three,
Glorious Trinity,
Wisdom, Love, Might—
Boundless as ocean's tide,
Rolling in fullest pride,
Through the world far and wide
Let there be light!

Septuagesima Sunday.

Hymn 61.   II.   MERTON COLLEGE.

IN the Name of God the Father,
  In the Name of God the Son,
In the Name of God the Spirit,
  One in Three, and Three in One,
In the Name which highest angels
  Speak not ere they veil their face,
Crying—Holy! Holy! Holy!
  Come we to this sacred place.

Here in figure represented,
  See the Passion once again,
Here behold the Lamb most Holy
  As for our redemption slain ;
Here the Saviour's Body broken,
  Here the Blood which Jesus shed,
Mystic Food of life eternal,
  See for our refreshment spread.

Here shall highest praise be offered,
  Here shall meekest prayers be poured,
Here with body, soul, and spirit,
  God Incarnate be adored.
Holy Jesu! for Thy coming
  May Thy love our hearts prepare ;
Thine we fain would have them wholly,
  Enter, Lord, and tarry there.

Septuagesima Sunday.

C OME, la'bour on!
  Who dares stand idle on the har'vest plain?
While all around him waves the gold'en grain,
And to each servant does the Mas'ter say,
  "Go work' to day!"

  Come, la'bour on!
Claim the high calling angels can'not share,—
To young and old the Gospel-glad'ness bear:
Redeem the time; its hours too swift'ly fly,
  The night' draws nigh.

Come, la'bour on !
The labourers are few, the field is wide,
New stations must be filled, and blanks' supplied ;
From voices distant far, or near' at home,
The call' is, " Come !"

Come, la'bour on !
The enemy is watching, night' and day,
To sow the tares, to snatch the seed' away.
While we in sleep our duty have' forgot,
He slum'bered not.

Come, la'bour on !
Away with gloomy doubts and faith'less fear !
No arm so weak but may do ser'vice here ;
By feeblest agents can our God' fulfil
His right'eous will.

Come, la'bour on !
No time for rest, till glows the west'ern sky,
While the long shadows o'er our path'way lie,
And a glad sound comes with the set'ting sun,—
" Servants', well done ! "

Come, la'bour on !
The toil is pleasant, the reward' is sure,
Blessed are those who to the end' endure ;
How full their joy, how deep their rest' shall be,
O Lord', with Thee !

Septuagesima Sunday.

Hymn 63.   IV.   GROSVENOR.

PRAISE the Lord of heaven,
    Praise Him in the height,
Praise Him, all ye angels,
    Praise Him, stars and light :
Praise Him, skies and waters,
    Which above the skies
When His word commanded
    Did established rise.

Praise the Lord, ye fountains
    Of the deeps and seas,
Rocks and hills, and mountains,
    Cedars, and all trees :
Praise Him, clouds and vapours,
    Snow and hail, and fire,
Stormy wind, fulfilling
    Only His desire.

Praise Him, fowls and cattle,
    Princes and all kings :
Praise Him, men and maidens,
    All created things :
For the Name of God is
    Excellent alone
Over earth His footstool,
    Over heaven His throne.

Sexagesima Sunday.

Hymn 64.   BABYLON STREAMS.

O THOU, at whose divine command
Good seed is sown in every land,
Thine Holy Ghost to us impart,
And for Thy Word prepare each heart.

Not among thorns of worldly thought,
Nor soon by passing plunderers caught,
Nor lacking depth the root to feed,
May we receive Thy Spirit's seed;

But may it, while Thy sowers toil,
Fall in a good and honest soil;
And springing up from firmest root,
With patience bear abundant fruit.

Seragesima Sunday.

THE heaven of heavens cannot contain
  The Universal Lord;
Yet He in humble hearts will deign
  To dwell and be adored.

Where'er ascends the sacrifice
  Of fervent praise and prayer,
Or on the earth, or in the skies,
  The heaven of God is there.

His presence there is spread abroad
  Through realms, through worlds unknown;
Who seeks the mercies of his God
  Is ever near His Throne.

Septagesima Sunday.

Hymn 66.   III.   MUNDEN.

HE who once in righteous vengeance
 Whelmed the world beneath the flood,
Once again in mercy cleansed it
 With His own most precious blood,
  Coming from His throne on high
  On the bitter Cross to die.

O the wisdom of the Eternal!
 O the depth of Love Divine!
O the sweetness of that mercy
 Which in Jesus Christ doth shine!
  We were sinners doomed to die,
  Jesus paid our penalty.

When before the Judge we tremble,
 Conscious of His broken laws,
May His blood in that dread moment
 Cry aloud and plead our cause,
  Bid our fears for ever cease,
  Be our pardon and our peace.

Prince and Author of salvation,
 Lord of majesty supreme,
Jesu, praise to Thee be given
 By the world Thou didst redeem:
  Glory to the Father be,
  And the Spirit, one with Thee.

Sexagesima Sunday.

Hymn 67.　　　　　　　IV.　　　　　　　WERNER.

NOT in any thing we do,
    Thought that's pure, or word that's true,
Saviour, would we put our trust :
Frail as vapour, vile as dust,
All that flatters we disown :
Righteousness is Thine alone.

Though we underwent for Thee
Perils of the land and sea,
Though we cast our lives away,
Dying for Thee day by day,
Boast we never of our own :
Grace and strength are Thine alone.

Native cumberers of the ground,
All our fruit from Thee is found :
Grafted in Thine olive, Lord,
New-begotten by Thy word,
All we have is Thine alone :
Life and power are not our own.

And when Thy returning voice
Calls Thy faithful to rejoice,
When the countless throng to Thee
Cast their crown of victory,
We will sing before the Throne,
" Thine the glory, not our own !"

Quinquagesima Sunday.

THOU who on that wondrous journey
Sett'st Thy face to die,
By Thy holy meek example
Teach us Charity!

Thou who that dread cup of suffering
Didst not put from Thee,
O most loving of the loving,
Give us Charity!

Thou who reignest, bright in glory,
On God's throne on high,
O that we may share Thy triumph,
Grant us Charity!

Send us Faith, that trusts Thy promise,
Hope, with upward eye,
But more blest than both, and greater,
Send us Charity!

Quinquagesima Sunday.

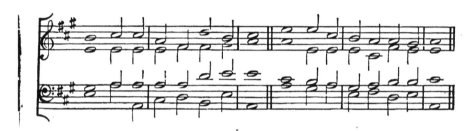

JESUS, where'er Thy people meet,
  There they behold Thy mercy-seat;
Where'er they seek Thee, Thou art found,
And every place is hallowed ground.

For Thou, within no walls confined,
Inhabitest the humblest mind;
Such ever bring Thee where they come,
And going take Thee to their home.

Dear Shepherd of Thy chosen few,
Thy former mercies here renew;
Here to our waiting hearts proclaim
The sweetness of Thy saving Name.

Lord, we are few, but Thou art near;
Nor short Thine arm, nor deaf Thine ear;
O rend the heavens, come quickly down,
And make *a thousand* hearts Thine own!

Quinquagesima Sunday.

R EJOICE, though storms assail thee:
    Rejoice, when skies are bright;
Rejoice, though round thy pathway
    Is spread the gloom of night:
If the good hope be in thee
    That all at last is well,
Then let thy happy spirit
    With joyful feelings swell!

Look back on early childhood,
    And let thy soul rejoice!
Who then upheld thy goings,
    And tuned thy feeble voice?
Look back on youth's gay visions,
    When life one glory seemed:
Who poured those rays of gladness
    Which on thy prospect beamed?

Recall the hours of anguish,
    And let thy soul rejoice,
Though wave on wave of sorrow
    Rush on with fearful noise:
Was not the Bow of Promise
    Still seen amidst the gloom,
Shedding its hallowed lustre
    E'en round the silent tomb?

Rejoice, rejoice for ever,
    Though earthly friends be gone!
For silently and swiftly
    The wheels of time roll on;
And still they bear thee forward,
    Nearer that happy shore,
Where the triumphant song is,
    " Rejoice for evermore!"

Quinquagesima Sunday.

IV. ST. THOMAS.

TAKE, O Lord, my faithless heart,
Make its choice the better part,
Break its chains and set it free,
Take and seal it, Lord, to Thee.

Though Thou turn my joy to tears,
Faith to doubt, and hope to fears :
Stern though be the summons home,
Still, Lord, let the summons come.

Should'st Thou bid me lay aside
All that fosters earthly pride,
Let me walk the lowly way,
If Thine arm may be my stay.

Should Thy chastening will require
All that feeds mine eyes' desire,
Take it, Lord, if in its place
Shine the brightness of Thy face.

Seal then, Lord, my heart to Thee,
Set it for Thy service free :
Life and joy are truly mine,
If whate'er I have is Thine.

Ash Wednesday.

BURFORD.

TURN not, O Lord, Thy face from me,
  Who tremble at Thy feet,
Lamenting sore my sinful life
  Before Thy mercy-seat.

O call me not to strict account,
  Thou who my faults canst tell :
What I have been, and what I am,
  O Lord, Thou know'st it well.

The circumstances of my crimes,
  Their number, and their kind ;
Thou know'st them all, and more, much more,
  Than I can call to mind.

Mercy, good Lord, mercy I ask :
  This is the total sum :
For mercy, Lord, is all my suit ;
  Lord, let Thy mercy come.

First Sunday in Lent.

CULROSS.

JESUS our Lord, who tempted wast
  In all points like as we;
And didst achieve in that dread fight
  Undoubted victory;

Teach us, when angered at our lot
  Our faithless souls repine,
Man liveth not by bread alone,
  But every word divine.

When we would rush on danger's point,
  And dare the lifted sword,
Speak in our ears the warning voice,
  "Thou shalt not tempt the Lord."

And when deceived by pride or power,
  Earth's idols we espouse,
Teach us that Thou art God alone,
  And on us are Thy vows.

Thus shall we more than conquerors
  With Thee pass through the strife;
And angels come and minister
  Around the heirs of life.

First Sunday in Lent.

FORTY days and forty nights
 Thou wast fasting in the wild :
Forty days and forty nights
 Tempted, and yet undefiled.

Sunbeams scorching all the day :
 Chilly dew-drops nightly shed :
Prowling beasts about Thy way,
 Stones Thy pillow, earth Thy bed.

Shall we not Thy sorrow share,
 And from earthly joys abstain,
Fasting with unceasing prayer,
 Glad with Thee to suffer pain ?

And if Satan vexing sore
 Flesh or spirit should assail,
Thou, his Vanquisher before,
 Grant we may not faint nor fail.

So shall we have peace divine,
 Holier gladness ours shall be :
Round us too shall angels shine,
 Such as ministered to Thee.

First Sunday in Lent.

Hymn 75.   **III.**   NANTES.

I LAY my sins on Jesus,
    The spotless Lamb of God,
He bears them all, and frees us
    From the accursed load.
I lay my wants on Jesus;
    All fulness dwells in Him;
He heals all my diseases;
    He doth my soul redeem.

I lay my griefs on Jesus,
    My burdens and my cares:
He from them all releases,
    And all my sorrows shares.
I love the Name of Jesus,
    Immanuel, Christ, the Lord:
Like fragrance on the breezes
    His Name abroad is poured.

I long to be like Jesus,
    Meek, loving, lowly, mild:
I long to be like Jesus,
    The Father's Holy Child:
I long to be with Jesus,
    Amid the heavenly throng,
To sing, with saints, His praises,
    To hear the angels' song.

Hymn 76.   IV.   ST. CLEMENT.

G OD of my life, to Thee I call,
   Afflicted at Thy feet I fall :
When the great water-floods prevail,
Leave not my trembling heart to fail.

Friend of the friendless and the faint,
Where should I lodge my deep complaint ?
Where but with Thee, whose open door
Invites the helpless and the poor ?

Did ever mourner plead with Thee,
And Thou refuse that mourner's plea ?
Does not the word still fixed remain,
That none shall seek Thy face in vain ?

Poor though I am, despised, forgot,
Yet God, my God, forgets me not :
And he is safe, and must succeed,
For whom the Lord vouchsafes to plead.

Second Sunday in Lent.

Hymn 77.   I.   MANCHESTER.

O HELP us, Lord! each hour of need
   Thy heavenly succour give;
Help us in thought, and word, and deed,
   Each hour on earth we live!

O help us when our spirits bleed
   With contrite anguish sore;
And when our hearts are cold and dead,
   O help us, Lord, the more!

O help us, through the prayer of faith,
   More firmly to believe;
For still, the more the servant hath,
   The more shall he receive.

O help us, Jesus, from on high!
   We know no help but Thee:
O help us so to live and die,
   As Thine in heaven to be!

Second Sunday in Lent.

Hymn 78.　　　　　　　　　II.　　　　　　　RICHMOND.

O LORD, Thou knowest all the snares
　　That round our pathway be,
Thou know'st that both our joys and cares
　Come between us and Thee :
Thou know'st that our infirmity
　In Thee alone is strong :
To Thee for help and strength we fly :
　O let us not go wrong!

O bear us up, protect us now
　In dark temptation's hour :
For Thou wert born of woman, Thou
　Hast felt the tempter's power :
All sinless, Thou canst feel for these
　Who strive and suffer long :
But O, midst all our cares and woes,
　Still let us not go wrong.

Second Sunday in Lent.

Hymn 79.   III.   LEONI.

BEHOLD the Lamb of God!
   Behold, believe, and live:
Behold His all-atoning blood,
    And life receive.
Look from thyself to Him,
   Behold Him on the tree:
What though the eye of faith be dim?
    He looks on Thee.

That meek, that languid eye,
   Turns from Himself away:
Invites the trembling sinner nigh,
    And bids him stay.
Stay with Him near the tree,
   Stay with Him near the tomb:
Stay till the risen Lord you see,
    Stay, till He come.

Hymn 80.   IV.   LUSTRA SEX.

WHEN our heads are bowed with woe,
   When our bitter tears o'erflow ;
When we mourn the lost, the dear,
Gracious Son of Mary, hear !

Thou our throbbing flesh hast worn,
Thou our mortal griefs hast borne,
Thou hast shed the human tear :
Gracious Son of Mary, hear !

When the sullen death-bell tolls
For our own departed souls ;
When our final doom is near,
Gracious Son of Mary, hear !

Thou hast bowed the dying head ;
Thou the blood of life hast shed ;
Thou hast filled a mortal bier :
Gracious Son of Mary, hear !

When the heart is sad within
With the thought of all its sin ;
When the spirit shrinks with fear,
Gracious Son of Mary, hear !

Thou the shame, the grief hast known,
Though the sins were not Thine own,
Thou hast deigned their load to bear,
Gracious Son of Mary, hear !

Hymn 81.   I.   WINDSOR.

WHEN, rising from the bed of death,
    O'erwhelmed with guilt and fear,
I see my Maker face to face,
    O how shall I appear?

If yet while pardon may be found
    And mercy may be sought,
My heart with inward horror shrinks
    And trembles at the thought ;

When Thou, O Lord, shalt stand disclosed
    In majesty severe,
And sit in judgment on my soul,
    O how shall I appear?

But Thou hast told the troubled soul,
    That doth her sins lament,
Of Him who suffered unto death,
    Her sufferings to prevent.

Then why, my soul, should'st thou despair
    Full pardon to procure,
Since Christ, the Lord of Glory, died
    To make that pardon sure?

Third Sunday in Lent.

Hymn 82. II. MUSGROVE.

GOD of my salvation, hear,
  And help me to believe;
Simply do I now draw near,
  Thy blessing to receive.
Full of guilt, alas! I am,
  But to Thy wounds for refuge flee;
Friend of sinners! spotless Lamb!
  Thy Blood was shed for me.

Standing now as newly slain,
  To Thee I lift mine eye;
Balm of all my grief and pain,
  Thy Blood is always nigh;
Now as yesterday the same
  Thou art, and wilt for ever be;
Friend of sinners! spotless Lamb!
  Thy Blood was shed for me.

Nothing have I, Lord, to pay,
  Nor can Thy grace procure;
Empty send me not away,
  For I, Thou know'st, am poor:
Dust and ashes is my name,
  My all is sin and misery:
Friend of sinners! spotless Lamb!
  Thy Blood was shed for me.

No good work, or word, or thought,
  Bring I to gain Thy grace;
Pardon I accept unbought,
  Thy proffer I embrace;
Coming, as at first I came,
  To take, and not bestow on Thee;
Friend of sinners! spotless Lamb!
  Thy Blood was shed for me.

Third Sunday in Lent.

Hymn 83. III. BEDFORD (Minor).

L ORD, when we bend before Thy throne,
    And our confessions pour,
Teach us to feel the sins we own,
    And hate what we deplore.

Our broken spirits pitying see,
    And penitence impart:
Then let a kindling ray from Thee
    Beam hope upon the heart.

When we disclose our wants in prayer,
    May we our wills resign:
And not a thought our bosom share
    That is not wholly Thine.

Let faith each meek petition fill,
    And waft it to the skies:
And teach our hearts 'tis goodness still
    That grants it, or denies.

Third Sunday in Lent.

Hymn 84.   IV.   MARTYRS'.

WHEN wounded sore the stricken soul
    Lies bleeding and unbound,
One only hand, a piercèd hand,
    Can salve the sinner's wound.

When sorrow swells the laden breast,
    And tears of anguish flow,
One only heart, a broken heart,
    Can feel the sinner's woe.

When penitence has wept in vain
    Over some foul dark spot,
One only stream, a stream of blood,
    Can wash away the blot.

'Tis Jesus' blood that washes white,
    His hand that brings relief,
His heart that's touched with all our joys
    And feeleth for our grief.

Lift up Thy bleeding hand, O Lord;
    Unseal that cleansing tide;
We have no shelter from our sin,
    But in Thy wounded side.

Fourth Sunday in Lent.

Hymn 85.   PRAYER.

H AVE mercy, Lord, O Lord, forgive ;
  Let the repenting sinner live ;
Is not Thy mercy great and free ?
May not the sinner trust in Thee ?

Wash us from all our sins, O God,
In Thy dear Son's atoning blood ;
Hear those who come before Thy throne,
Pleading His merits, not their own.

Though we have grieved Thy Spirit, Lord,
His gracious presence still afford ;
And still salvation's joys impart,
To heal the broken contrite heart.

A broken heart, O God our King,
Is all the sacrifice we bring ;
Thou, God of Grace, wilt not despise
A broken heart in sacrifice.

Fourth Sunday in Lent.

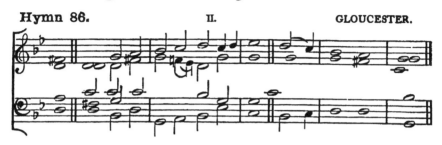

JESU, Thou art my Righteousness,
   For all my sins were Thine ;
Thy death hath bought of God my peace,
   Thy life hath made Him mine.

For ever here my rest shall be,
   Close to Thy bleeding side ;
This all my hope, and all my plea,
   For me the Saviour died.

My dying Saviour and my God,
   Fountain for guilt and sin,
Sprinkle me ever with Thy blood,
   And cleanse and keep me clean.

The atonement of Thy blood apply
   Till faith to sight improve ;
Till hope in full fruition die,
   And all my soul be love.

Fourth Sunday in Lent.

JUST as I am, without one plea
But that Thy blood was shed for me,
And that Thou bidd'st me come to Thee,
　　O Lamb of God, I come!

Just as I am, and waiting not
To rid my soul of one dark blot,
To Thee, whose blood can cleanse each spot,
　　O Lamb of God, I come!

Just as I am, though tossed about
With many a conflict, many a doubt,
Fightings and fears within, without,
　　O Lamb of God, I come!

Just as I am, poor, wretched, blind,
Sight, riches, healing of the mind,
Yea, all I need, in Thee to find,
　　O Lamb of God, I come!

Just as I am, Thou wilt receive,
Wilt welcome, pardon, cleanse, relieve:
Because Thy promise I believe,
　　O Lamb of God, I come!

Just as I am (Thy love unknown
Has broken every barrier down),
Now to be Thine, yea Thine alone,
　　O Lamb of God, I come!

Just as I am, of that free love
The breadth, length, depth, and height to prove,
Here for a season, then above,
　　O Lamb of God, I come!

Fourth Sunday in Lent.

Hymn 88. IV. DANTZICK.

Major, for verses 1, 4, 5.

Minor, for verses 2, 3.

L ORD of mercy and of might,
 Maker, Teacher Infinite,
Of mankind the life and light,
 Jesus, hear and save.

Who when sin's tremendous doom
Gave creation to the tomb,
Didst not scorn the Virgin's womb,
 Jesus, hear and save.

Mighty monarch, Saviour mild,
Humbled to a mortal child,
Captive, beaten, bound, reviled,
 Jesus, hear and save.

Throned above celestial things,
Borne aloft on angels' wings,
Lord of Lords and King of Kings,
 Jesus, hear and save.

Who shall yet return from high,
Robed in might and majesty,
Hear us, help us when we cry;
 Jesus, hear and save.

Hymn 89. 1. HYMNUS EUCHARISTICUS.

SAVIOUR, I lift my trembling eyes
　　To that bright seat where, placed on high,
The great, the atoning Sacrifice,
　　For me, for all, is ever nigh.

Be Thou my guard on peril's brink ;
　　Be Thou my guide through weal or woe ;
And teach me of Thy cup to drink,
　　And make me in Thy path to go.

For what is earthly change or loss ?
　　Thy promises are still my own :
The feeblest frame may bear Thy cross,
　　The lowliest spirit share Thy Throne.

Fifth Sunday in Lent.

NOW let us join with hearts and tongues,
  And emulate the angels' songs;
Yea, sinners may address their King
In songs that angels cannot sing.

They praise the Lamb who once was slain,
But we can add a higher strain;
Not only say, He suffered thus,
But that He suffered all for us.

Jesus, who passed the angels by,
Assumed our flesh to bleed and die;
And still He makes it His abode;
As Man He fills the throne of God.

Our next of kin, our Brother now,
Is He to whom the angels bow;
They join with us to praise His Name.
But we the nearest interest claim.

Fifth Sunday in Lent.

Hymn 91.   III.   MAYENNE.

ROCK of Ages, cleft for me,
    Let me hide myself in Thee :
Let the water and the blood,
From Thy riven side which flowed,
Be of sin the double cure,
Save from guilt and make me pure.

Not the labours of my hands
Can fulfil Thy law's demands :
Could my zeal no respite know,
Could my tears for ever flow,
All for sin could not atone :
Thou must save, and Thou alone.

Nothing in my hand I bring,
Simply to Thy Cross I cling :
Naked, come to Thee for dress :
Helpless, look to Thee for grace :
Foul, I to the fountain fly :
Wash me, Saviour, or I die.

While I draw this fleeting breath,
When my eye-strings break in death,
When I soar through tracts unknown,
See Thee on Thy judgment-throne :
Rock of Ages, cleft for me,
Let me hide myself in Thee.

Fifth Sunday in Lent.

O THOU to whose all-searching sight
   The darkness shineth as the light,
Search, prove my heart : it pants for Thee :
O burst these bands, and set it free.

Wash out its stains, refine its dross :
Nail my affections to the Cross :
Hallow each thought, let all within
Be clean, as Thou my Lord art clean.

If in this darksome wild I stray,
Be Thou my Light, be Thou my Way :
No foes, no violence I fear,
No fraud, while Thou my God art near.

When rising floods my soul o'erflow,
When sinks my heart in waves of woe,
Jesu, Thy timely aid impart,
And raise my head, and cheer my heart.

If rough and thorny be the way,
My strength proportion to my day :
Till toil and grief and pain shall cease,
Where all is calm and joy and peace.

Sunday next before Easter.

I. ALL SOULS.

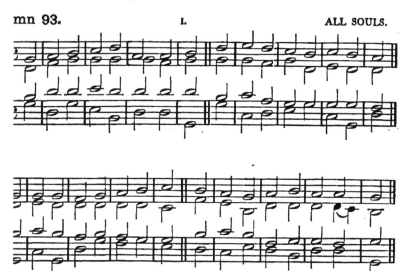

R IDE on, ride on in Majesty!
Hark! all the tribes Hosanna cry;
O Saviour meek, pursue Thy road,
With palms and scattered garments strowed.

Ride on, ride on in Majesty!
In lowly pomp ride on to die:
O Christ, Thy triumphs now begin
O'er captive death and conquered sin.

Ride on, ride on in Majesty!
The angel armies of the sky
Look down with sad and wondering eyes
To see the approaching Sacrifice.

Ride on, ride on in Majesty!
In lowly pomp ride on to die:
Bow Thy meek Head to mortal pain,
Then take, O God, Thy power. and reign.

Sunday next before Easter.

WHEN I survey the wondrous Cross,
   On which the Prince of Glory died,
My richest gain I count but loss,
   And pour contempt on all my pride.

Forbid it, Lord, that I should boast,
   Save in the death of Christ my God :
All the vain things that charm me most
   I sacrifice them to His Blood.

See from His head, His hands, His feet,
   Sorrow and love flow mingled down :
Did e'er such love and sorrow meet,
   Or thorns compose so rich a crown ?

Were the whole realm of nature mine,
   That were an offering far too small ;
Love so amazing, so divine,
   Demands my life, my soul, my all.

Sunday next before Easter.

" LO, I come to do Thy will : "
　　When the Father's only Son
Came this promise to fulfil,
　　Then Salvation's work was done.

Just, He for the unjust died,
　　So to bring their souls to God,
Sheltered in His wounded side,
　　Washed in His atoning Blood.

What to His are all my pains
　　But the smallest balance-dust ?
Mine, whose soul is full of stains :
　　He, the Holy One and Just?

But His sufferings are o'er :
　　He hath entered into Peace :
Passing was the Cross He bore,
　　While its virtues never cease.

Sunday next before Easter.

SEE what unbounded zeal and love
    Inflamed the Saviour's breast,
When stedfast towards Jerusalem
    His urgent way He prest.
Good-will to man, and zeal for God
    His every thought engross:
He longs to be baptized with blood,
    He thirsts to reach the Cross.

With all His sufferings full in view,
    And woes to us unknown,
Forth to the work His spirit flew,
    'Twas Love that urged Him on:
By His obedience unto death
    See Paradise restored:
And fallen man brought face to face
    With His forgiving Lord.

Prepare us, Lord, to view Thy Cross,
    Who all our griefs hast borne;
To look on Thee, whom we have pierced,
    To look on Thee, and mourn:
While thus we mourn, may we rejoice,
    And as Thy Cross we see,
May each exclaim in faith and hope,
    " The Saviour died for me !"

Monday before Easter.

G LORY of Thy Father's face,
  Fountain deep of Love and Grace,
Who, Lord, can repay Thee thus,
As Thou gav'st Thyself for us?

What to Thee shall we reply,
Who for us didst bleed and die,
When Thou shalt the question make,
"What have ye done for My sake?"

Hard in heart, in action weak,
Lord, Thy grace divine we seek:
Set us from our bondage free;
Draw us, and we follow Thee.

Tuesday before Easter.

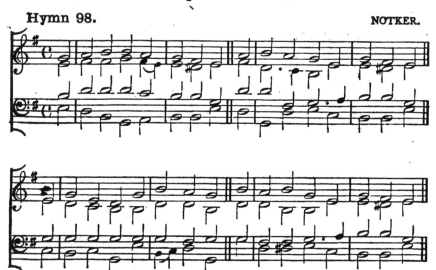

LORD Jesu, when we stand afar
 And gaze upon Thy holy Cross,
In love of Thee and scorn of self,
 O may we count the world as loss.

When we behold Thy bleeding wounds,
 And the rough way that Thou hast trod,
Make us to hate the load of sin
 That lay so heavy on our God.

O holy Lord, uplifted high
 With outstretched arms, in mortal woe,
Embracing in Thy wondrous love
 The sinful world that lies below,

Give us an ever-living faith,
 To gaze beyond the things we see ;
And in the mystery of Thy death
 Draw us and all men unto Thee.

Wednesday before Easter.

BOHEMIA.

I N the hour of trial,
  Jesus, pray for me,
Lest, by base denial
  I depart from Thee:
When Thou seest me waver,
  With a look recall,
Nor, for fear or favour,
  Suffer me to fall.

With its witching pleasures
  Would this vain world charm:
Or its sordid treasures
  Spread, to work me harm:
Bring to my remembrance
  Sad Gethsemane,
Or, in darker semblance,
  Cross-crowned Calvary.

If with sore affliction
  Thou in love chastise,
Pour Thy benediction
  On the sacrifice:
Then upon Thine altar
  Freely offered up,
Though the flesh may falter,
  Faith shall drink the cup.

When in dust and ashes
  To the grave I sink,
While heaven's glory flashes
  O'er the shelving brink:
On Thy truth relying,
  Through that mortal strife,
Lord, receive me, dying,
  To eternal life.

Hymn 100.   PRESBURG.

G O to dark Gethsemane,
  Ye that feel the Tempter's power :
Your Redeemer's conflict see,
  Watch with Him the bitter hour :
    Turn not from His cries away :
    Learn of Jesus Christ to pray.

Follow to the judgment hall,
  See the Lord of life arraigned :
See the wormwood and the gall :
  See the pangs that He sustained :
    Shun not suffering, shame, or loss :
    Learn of Him to bear the cross.

Follow Him to Calvary's hill,
  There, adoring at His feet,
See Him do the Father's will,
  See the sacrifice complete :
    " It is finished !" hear Him cry.
    Learn of Jesus Christ to die.

Good Friday.

CLEFT are the rocks, the earth doth quake,
    The slumberers of the grave awake;
The temple's veil is rent in twain :
For Christ our sacrifice is slain,
And bears of sin and death the pain.

Lo ! nature's face of beaming light
She veils in darkness at the sight
Of Him, her God, the Crucified :
'Tis man alone that dares deride
The Saviour who for him hath died.

The Mighty One, the Son of God,
Hath humbly kissed affliction's rod,
That by His stripes we might be healed
Our pardon by His blood be sealed,
And boundless mercy stand revealed.

Oh let us cast each vice away
Which thus the Son of God could slay !
With contrite heart and weeping eye
Behold the Saviour's Cross on high,
And every sin and folly fly !

So may we join the song of love
Which saints and angels sing above :
All honour, glory, praise to Thee,
Which wert, and art, and art to be,
The Lamb, slain from eternity !

Good Friday.

H AIL that head with sorrows bowing,
   Crowned with thorns, with anguish flowing ;
And that body pierced and shaken,
Mocked of man, of God forsaken,
    Marred beyond the sons of men ;

By Thy death of life the giver,
When we suffer, O deliver !
In our sorrow and our weakness,
Thou who didst prevail by meekness,
    Think upon Thy woes again !

When the hour of death is near us,
Be Thou present, Lord, to cheer us :
In that time of fear and sadness
Tarry not, our Help and Gladness,
    Saviour of the sons of men !

When our latest breath is failing,
Be Thy Spirit all-prevailing :
When the Tempter's wiles shall prove us,
Shew Thy sacred sign above us,
    Hold us, save us, free us then !

Good Friday.

SEE the destined day arise !
　　See, a willing Sacrifice
To redeem our fatal loss,
Jesus hangs upon the Cross.

Jesus, who but Thou had borne,
Lifted on that tree of scorn,
Every pang and bitter throe,
Finishing Thy life of woe ?

Who but Thou had dared to drain,
Steeped in gall, the cup of pain ?
And with tender body bear
Thorns, and nails, and piercing spear?

Thence poured forth the water flowed,
Mingled from Thy side with blood :
Sign to all attesting eyes
Of the finished Sacrifice.

Holy Jesus, grant us grace,
In that Sacrifice to place
All our trust for life renewed,
Pardoned sin, and promised good.

Good Friday.

WE sing the praise of Him who died,
  Of Him who died upon the Cross;
The sinner's hope let men deride,
  For this we count the world but loss.

Inscribed upon the Cross we see
  In shining letters, God is Love;
He bears our sins upon the tree,
  He brings us mercy from above.

The Cross! it takes our guilt away;
  It holds the fainting spirit up;
It cheers with hope the gloomy day,
  And sweetens every bitter cup;

It makes the coward spirit brave,
  And nerves the feeble arm for fight:
It takes its terror from the grave,
  And gilds the bed of death with light;

The balm of life, the cure of woe,
  The measure and the pledge of Love;
The sinner's refuge here below,
  The angels' theme in heaven above.

Easter Even.

DELAWARE.

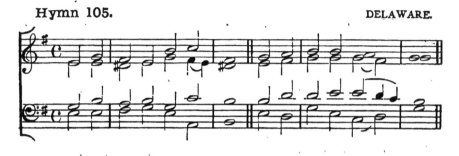

I N the tomb behold He lies
    Who the dead awaketh :
Christ, our stricken Sacrifice,
    Of sweet rest partaketh.

Fear we then no more the gloom
    Of Death's narrow dwelling ;
Jesus died ! the wondering tomb
    Of His praise is telling.

Vainly shall His foes rejoice :
    Vainly Death detain Him :
Lazarus heard His wakening voice :
    What shall then restrain Him ?

What shall bind His conquering arm
    Who the mountains rendeth,
And, that He may Death disarm,
    To the tomb descendeth ?

Easter Day.

WORGAN'S.

JESUS CHRIST is risen to-day, . . Hallelujah.

Our triumphant holiday ; . . . . Hallelujah.

Who did once upon the Cross . . . . Hallelujah.

Suffer to redeem our loss. . . . . . . Hallelujah.

Hymns of praise then let us sing . . . . Hallelujah.

Unto Christ our heavenly King ; . . . . Hallelujah.

Who endured both Cross and grave, . . . Hallelujah.

Sinners to redeem and save. . . . . . Hallelujah.

But the pains which He endured . . . . Hallelujah.

Our salvation have procured : . . . . . Hallelujah.

Now above the skies He's King, ... Hallelujah.

Where the angels ever sing . . . . . Hallelujah.

Easter Day.

II. ELVEY.

CHRIST the Lord is risen to-day,
Sons of men and angels say :
Raise your joys and triumphs high,
Sing, ye heavens, and earth reply.
Love's redeeming work is done,
Fought the fight, the battle won :
Lo! our Sun's eclipse is o'er ;
Lo! He sets in blood no more.

Vain the stone, the watch, the seal ;
Christ hath burst the gates of hell !
Death in vain forbids His rise ;
Christ hath opened Paradise.
Lives again our glorious King ;
Where, O Death, is now thy sting ?
Once He died, our souls to save :
Where thy victory, O Grave ?

Soar we now where Christ has led,
Following our exalted Head ;
Made like Him, like Him we rise ;
Ours the Cross, the grave, the skies.
What though once we perished all
Partners in our parents' fall ?
Second life we all receive,
In our Heavenly Adam live.

Easter Day.

Hymn 108.　　　　　　　**III.**　　　　　　**MERTON COLLEGE.**

HALLELUJAH, Hallelujah! Hearts to heaven and voices raise :
Sing to God a hymn of gladness, sing to God a hymn of praise.
He who on the Cross a victim for the world's salvation bled,
Jesus Christ, the King of Glory, now is risen from the dead.

Now the iron bars are broken, Christ from death to life is born,
Glorious life, and life immortal, on this holy Easter morn :
Christ has triumphed, and we conquer by His mighty enterprise,
We with Christ to Life Eternal by His Resurrection rise.

Christ is risen, Christ the first fruits of the holy harvest field,
Which will all its full abundance at His second coming yield :
Men the golden ears of harvest with their heads before Him wave,
Ripened by His glorious sunshine, from the furrows of the grave.

Christ is risen, we are risen : shed upon us heavenly grace,
Rain and dew and streams of glory from the brightness of Thy face,
That we, with our hearts in heaven, here on earth may fruitful be,
And by angel-hands be gathered, and be ever, Lord, with Thee.

Easter Day.

THIS is the day the Lord hath made;
　　He calls the hours His own:
Let heaven rejoice, let earth be glad,
　　And praise surround the throne.

To-day He rose and left the dead,
　　And Satan's empire fell:
To-day the saints His triumphs spread,
　　And all His wonders tell.

Hosanna to the anointed King,
　　To David's holy Son:
Help us, O Lord; descend and bring
　　Salvation from the throne.

Blest be the Lord who comes to men
　　With messages of grace,
Who comes in God His Father's name,
　　To save our sinful race.

Hosanna in the highest strains
　　The Church on earth can raise:
The highest heavens in which He reigns
　　Shall give Him nobler praise.

Monday in Easter Week.

Hal - le - lu - jah.

J ESUS lives! no longer now
Can thy terrors, Death, appal us:
Jesus lives! by this we know,
Thou, O Grave, canst not enthral us.
Hallelujah!

Jesus lives! for us He died,
Then, alone to Jesus living,
Pure in heart may we abide,
Glory to our Saviour giving.
Hallelujah!

Jesus lives! to Him the throne
Over all the world is given:
May we go where He is gone,
Rest and reign with Him in heaven.
Hallelujah!

Hymn 111.

ST. ALBINUS.

Hal - le - lu - jah.

J ESUS lives! henceforth is death
But the gate of life immortal:
This shall calm our trembling breath,
When we pass its gloomy portal.
Hallelujah!

Jesus lives! our hearts know well
Nought from us his soul shall sever:
Life, nor death, nor power of hell,
Tear us from His keeping ever.
Hallelujah!

Jesus lives! to Him the throne
Over all the world is given:
May we go where He is gone,
Rest and reign with Him in heaven.
Hallelujah!

First Sunday after Easter.

Hymn 112.   L.   IRONS.

JERUSALEM, my happy home,
   Name ever dear to me,
    When shall my labours have an end,
   Thy joys when shall I see?

When shall these eyes thy heaven-built walls
   And pearly gates behold?
Thy bulwarks of salvation strong,
   And streets of shining gold?

O when, thou city of my God,
   Shall I thy courts ascend,
Where congregations ne'er break up,
   And Sabbaths have no end?

Apostles, martyrs, prophets there
   Around my Saviour stand;
And all my friends in Christ below
   Shall join the glorious band.

Jerusalem, my happy home,
   When shall I come to thee?
Then shall my labours have an end,
   When I thy joys shall see.

First Sunday after Easter.

G IVE to our God immortal praise;
    Mercy and truth are all His ways:
Wonders of grace to God belong,
Repeat His mercies in your song.

He fills the sun with morning light,
He bids the moon direct the night:
His mercies ever shall endure,
When sun and moon shall shine no more.

He sent His Son with power to save
From guilt and darkness and the grave:
Wonders of grace to God belong,
Repeat His mercies in your song.

Through this vain world He guides our feet,
And leads us to His heavenly seat:
His mercies ever shall endure,
When this vain world shall be no more.

H OW bright those glorious spirits shine !
  Whence all their bright array ?
How came they to the blissful seats
  Of everlasting day ?

Lo, these are they from sufferings great
  Who came to realms of light :
And in the Blood of Christ they washed
  Those robes which shine so bright.

Now with triumphal palms they stand
  Before the throne so high,
And serve the God they love amidst
  The glories of the sky.

Hunger and thirst are felt no more,
  Nor sun with scorching ray :
God is their Sun, whose cheering beams
  Diffuse eternal day.

The Lamb who reigns upon the throne,
  Shall o'er them still preside,
Feed them with nourishment divine,
  And all their footsteps guide.

'Mid pastures green He'll lead His flock,
  Where living streams appear :
And God the Lord from every eye
  Shall *wipe off* every tear.

WE'VE no abiding city here :
    Then let us live as pilgrims do :
Let not the world our rest appear,
    But let us haste from all below.

We've no abiding city here :
    We seek a city out of sight :
Zion its name, the Lord is there,
    It shines with everlasting light.

Zion ! Jehovah is her strength ;
    Serene she smiles at all her foes ;
And weary travellers at length
    Within her sacred walls repose.

O sweet abode of peace and love,
    Where pilgrims freed from toil are blest !
Had I the pinions of a dove,
    I'd fly to thee, and be at rest.

Second Sunday after Easter.

Hymn 116.   I.   LONDON NEW.

THE God of love my Shepherd is,
    And He that doth me feed:
While He is mine, and I am His,
    What can I want or need?

He leads me to the tender grass,
    Where I both feed and rest:
Then to the streams that gently pass;
    In both I have the best.

Or if I stray, He doth convert,
    And bring my mind in frame;
And all this not for my desert,
    But for His holy Name.

Yea, in death's shady black abode
    Well may I walk, not fear;
For Thou art with me, and Thy rod
    To guide, Thy staff to bear.

Surely Thy sweet and wondrous love
    Shall measure all my days:
And as it never shall remove,
    So neither shall my praise.

Second Sunday after Easter.

Hymn 117.   II.   ALNWICK.

GREAT Prophet of my God,
  My tongue would bless Thy Name :
By Thee the joyful news
  Of our salvation came :
The joyful news of sins forgiven,
Of hell subdued, and peace with heaven.

Be Thou my Counsellor,
  My Pattern, and my Guide :
And through this desert land
  Still keep me near Thy side :
O let my feet ne'er run astray,
Nor rove, nor seek the crooked way.

I love my Shepherd's voice :
  His watchful eyes shall keep
My wandering soul among
  The thousands of His sheep ;
He feeds His flock, He calls their names,
His bosom bears the tender lambs.

Hymn 118.   III.   ST. GALL.

J ESUS, the Shepherd of the sheep
    Thy little flock in safety keep;
The flock for which Thou cam'st from heaven,
The flock for which Thy life was given.

O guard Thy sheep from beasts of prey,
And guide them that they never stray:
Cherish the young, sustain the old,
Let none be feeble in Thy fold.

Secure them from the scorching beam,
And lead them to the living stream:
In verdant pastures let them lie,
And watch them with a Shepherd's eye.

O may Thy sheep discern Thy voice,
And in its sacred sound rejoice:
From strangers may they ever flee,
And know no other guide but Thee.

Lord, bring Thy sheep that wander yet,
And let the number be complete:
Then let Thy flock from earth remove,
And occupy the fold above.

Second Sunday after Easter.

Hymn 119. IV. TRANBY.

THIS is not my place of resting,
  Mine's a city yet to come :
Onwards to it I am hasting,
  On to my eternal home.

In it all is light and glory,
  O'er it shines a nightless day :
Every trace of sin's sad story,
  All the curse has passed away.

There the Lamb our Shepherd leads us,
  By the streams of life along :
On the freshest pastures feeds us,
  Turns our sighing into song.

Soon we pass this desert dreary,
  Soon we bid farewell to pain :
Never more be sad or weary,
  Never, never sin again.

L 2

Third Sunday after Easter.

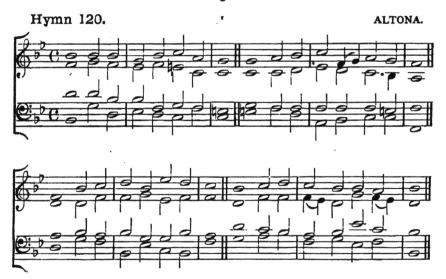

L ET me be with Thee where Thou art,
  My Saviour, my Eternal Rest :
Then only will this longing heart
  Be fully and for ever blest.

Let me be with Thee where Thou art,
  Thy unveiled glory to behold :
Then only will this wandering heart
  Cease to be treacherous, faithless, cold.

Let me be with Thee where Thou art,
  Where spotless saints Thy name adore :
Then only will this sinful heart
  Be evil and defiled no more.

Let me be with Thee where Thou art,
  Where none can die, where none remove :
Then neither death nor life will part
  Me from Thy presence and Thy love.

Third Sunday after Easter.

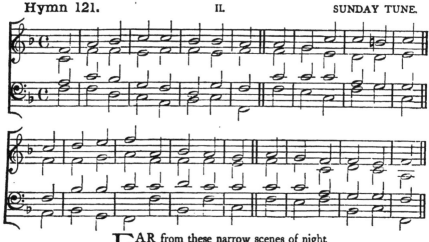

FAR from these narrow scenes of night
  Unbounded glories rise,
And realms of infinite delight,
  Unknown to mortal eyes.

There pain and sickness never come,
  And grief no more complains :
Health triumphs in immortal bloom,
  And endless pleasure reigns.

No cloud those blissful regions know,
  For ever bright and fair ;
For sin, the source of mortal woe,
  Can never enter there.

There no alternate night is known,
  Nor sun's faint sickly ray ;
But glory from the sacred Throne
  Spreads everlasting day.

The glorious Monarch there displays
  His beams of wondrous grace ;
His happy subjects sing His praise,
  And bow before His face.

O may the heavenly prospect fire
  Our hearts with ardent love,
Till wings of faith and strong desire
  Bear every thought above.

Third Sunday after Easter.

Hymn 122.   III.   ALTORF.

THE Lord of Might from Sinai's brow
  Gave forth His voice of thunder :
And Israel lay on earth below,
  Outstretched in fear and wonder :
Beneath His feet was pitchy night,
And at His left hand and His right
  The rocks were rent asunder.

The Lord of Love on Calvary,
  A meek and suffering stranger,
Upraised to heaven His languid eye
  In nature's hour of danger :
For us He bore the weight of woe,
For us He gave His blood to flow,
  And met His Father's anger.

The Lord of Love, the Lord of Might,
  The King of all created,
Shall back return to claim His right,
  On clouds of glory seated :
With trumpet-sound and angel-song,
And hallelujahs loud and long,
  O'er death and hell defeated.

Third Sunday after Easter.

Hymn 123.　　　　　　　IV.　　　　　　　OLD 25TH.

"FOR ever with the Lord!"
  Amen, so let it be:
Life from the dead is in that word,
  And immortality.
Here in the body pent,
  Absent from Him I roam:
Yet nightly pitch my moving tent
  A day's march nearer home.

My Father's house on high,
  Home of my soul, how near
At times to Faith's foreseeing eye
  Thy golden gates appear!
My thirsty spirit faints
  To reach the land I love,
The bright inheritance of saints,
  Jerusalem above!

I hear at morn and even,
  At noon and midnight hour,
The choral harmonies of heaven
  Earth's Babel tongues o'erpower.
"For ever with the Lord!"
  Father, if 'tis Thy will,
The promise of that faithful word,
  Ev'n here to me fulfil.

So, when my latest breath
  Shall rend the veil in twain,
By death I shall escape from death,
  And life eternal gain.
Knowing as I am known,
  How shall I love that word,
And oft repeat before the throne,
  "For ever with the Lord!"

Fourth Sunday after Easter.

Hymn 124. L. PARACLETE.

H OLY Ghost, the Comforter!
    Now from highest heaven appear,
Send Thy gracious radiance here.

Come to them who suffer dearth,
With Thy gifts of priceless worth,
Lighten all who dwell on earth.

Thou the heart's most precious guest,
Thou of comforters the best,
Give to us, the o'erladen, rest.

Blessed Sun of Grace ! o'er all
Faithful hearts, who on Thee call,
Let Thy joy and solace fall.

Cleanse us, Lord, from sinful stain,
O'er the parchéd heart O rain,
Heal the wounded from its pain.

Bend the stubborn will to Thine,
Melt the cold with fire divine,
Erring hearts aright incline.

Fourth Sunday after Easter.

IN the hour of my distress,
When temptations me oppress,
And when I my sins confess,
Sweet Spirit, comfort me.

When I lie within my bed,
Sick in heart and sick in head,
And with doubts disquieted,
Sweet Spirit, comfort me.

When the house doth sigh and weep,
And the world is drowned in sleep,
Yet mine eyes the watch do keep,
Sweet Spirit, comfort me.

When the tempter me pursu'th
With the sins of all my youth,
And reproves me for untruth,
Sweet Spirit, comfort me.

When the judgment is revealed,
And that opened which was sealed,
When to Thee I have appealed,
Sweet Spirit, comfort me.

Hymn 126.　　　　　　III.　　　　　BEAUMONT.

THY way, not mine, O Lord,
　However dark it be :
Lead me by Thine own hand,
　Choose out the path for me.

Smooth let it be or rough,
　It will be still the best ;
Winding or straight, it leads
　Right onward to Thy rest.

Take Thou my cup, and it
　With joy or sorrow fill,
As best to Thee may seem ;
　Choose Thou my good and ill ;

Choose Thou for me my friends,
　My sickness or my health ;
Choose Thou my cares for me,
　My poverty or wealth.

Not mine, not mine the choice
　In things or great or small ;
Be Thou my guide, my strength,
　My wisdom, and my all.

Hymn 127.   IV.   PRAGUE.

JESUS calls us o'er the tumult
  Of our life's wild restless sea ;
Day by day His sweet voice soundeth,
  Saying, "Christian, follow Me."

Jesus calls us from the worship
  Of the vain world's golden store,
From each idol that would keep us,
  Saying, "Christian, love Me more."

In our joys and in our sorrows,
  Days of toil and hours of ease,
Still He calls, in cares and pleasures,
  "Christian, love Me more than these."

Jesus calls us ! by Thy mercies,
  Saviour, may we hear Thy call,
Give our hearts to Thy obedience,
  Serve and love Thee best of all.

Fifth Sunday after Easter.

Hymn 128.

HYMN ON HEAVEN.

FOR thee, O dear dear country,
  Mine eyes their vigils keep :
For very love, beholding
  Thy happy name, they weep.
The mention of thy glory
  Is unction to the breast,
And medicine in sickness,
  And love, and life, and rest.

O one, O only mansion,
  O Paradise of Joy,
Where tears are ever banished,
  And smiles have no alloy ;
The Lamb is all thy splendour,
  The Crucified thy praise :
His laud and benediction
  Thy ransomed people raise.

O sweet and blessed country,
  The home of God's elect ;
O sweet and blessed country,
  That eager hearts expect !
Jesu, in mercy bring us
  To that dear land of rest :
Who art with God the Father,
  And Spirit, ever blest.

Fifth Sunday after Easter.

Hymn 129.   II.   ANNUE CHRISTE.

THERE is a blessed home
  Beyond this land of woe,
Where trials never come,
  Nor tears of sorrow flow:
Where faith is lost in sight.
  And patient hope is crowned,
And everlasting light
  Its glory throws around.

There is a land of peace,
  Good angels know it well:
Glad songs that never cease
  Within its portals swell;
Around its glorious throne
  Ten thousand saints adore
Christ, with the Father One,
  And Spirit, evermore.

Look up, ye saints of God,
  Nor fear to tread below
The path your Saviour trod,
  Of daily toil and woe.
Wait but a little while,
  In uncomplaining love,
His own most gracious smile
  Shall welcome you above.

Hymn 130.   III.   MELROSE.

WHEN I survey life's varied scene,
    Amid the darkest hours
Sweet rays of comfort shine between,
    And thorns are mixed with flowers.

Lord, teach me to adore Thy hand,
    From whence my comforts flow,
And let me, in this desert land,
    A glimpse of Canaan know.

And O, whate'er of earthly bliss
    Thy sovereign hand denies,
Accepted at Thy throne of grace,
    Let this petition rise :

Give me a calm, a thankful heart,
    From every murmur free ;
The blessings of Thy grace impart,
    And let me live to Thee.

Let the sweet hope that Thou art mine
    My path of life attend,
Thy presence through my journey shine,
    And bless its happy end.

Hymn 131.   IV.   CARLISLE.

THROUGH sorrow's path and danger's road,
    Amid the deepening gloom,
We soldiers of an injured King
    Are marching to the tomb.

Our labours done, securely laid
    In this our last retreat,
Unheeded o'er our silent dust
    The storms of life shall beat.

Yet not thus lifeless, thus inane,
    The vital spark shall lie,
For o'er life's wreck that spark shall rise
    To seek its kindred sky.

These ashes too, this little dust,
    Our Father's care shall keep,
Till the last angel rise, and break
    The long and dreary sleep.

Then love's soft dew o'er every eye
    Shall shed its mildest rays,
And the long-silent dust shall burst
    With shouts of endless praise.

M 2

Ascension Day.

TESCHNER.

LO! God to heaven ascendeth :
    Throughout its regions vast,
With shouts triumphant blendeth
    The trumpet's thrilling blast :
Sing praise with exultation,
    Sing praise to Christ the Lord :
King of each heathen nation,
    The God of Hosts adored.

With joy is heaven resounding,
    Christ's glad return to see :
Behold the saints surrounding
    The Lord, who set them free :
The cherub band rejoices,
    Bright myriads thronging come,
And loud seraphic voices
    Welcome Messiah home.

No more the way is hidden,
    Since Christ our Head arose ;
No more to man forbidden
    The road to heaven that goes.
Where Jesus Christ has entered,
    There may our hearts be found ;
There let our hopes be centred,
    Our journey thither bound.

Ascension Day.

HE is gone, and we remain
　　In this world of sin and pain;
In the void which He has left,
On this earth, of Him bereft:
We have still His work to do,
We can still His path pursue,
Seek Him both in friend and foe,
In ourselves His image shew.

He is gone, but we once more
Shall behold Him as before,
In the heaven of heavens, the same
As on earth He went and came;
In the many mansions there
Place for us He will prepare;
In that world unseen, unknown,
He and we may yet be one.

He is gone, but not in vain:
Wait, until He comes again;
He is risen, He is not here,
Far above this earthly sphere;
Evermore in heart and mind,
There our peace in Him we find;
To our own Eternal Friend,
Thitherward let us ascend.

Sunday after Ascension Day.

Hymn 134.   L.   SURSUM CORDA.

G O up, go up, my heart,
    Dwell with thy God above ;
For here thou canst not rest,
    Nor here give out thy love.

Go up, go up, my heart,
    Be not a trifler here ;
Ascend above these clouds,
    Dwell in a higher sphere.

Let not thy love flow out
    To things so soiled and dim ;
Go up to heaven and God,
    Take up thy love to Him.

Waste not thy precious stores
    On creature-love below :
To God that wealth belongs,
    On Him that wealth bestow.

Go up, reluctant heart,
    Take up thy rest above ;
Arise, earth-clinging thoughts ;
    Ascend, my lingering love.

Sunday after Ascension Day.

Hymn 135.　　　　　　　　　**II.**　　　　　　　**ST. GEORGE.**

THE Head that once was crowned
　　with thorns,
Is crowned with glory now ;
A royal diadem adorns
　The mighty Victor's brow.

The highest place that heaven affords
　Is His, is His by right,
The King of kings, and Lord of lords,
　And heaven's eternal Light.

The joy of all who dwell above,
　The joy of all below,
To whom He manifests His love,
　And grants His Name to know.

To them the Cross, with all its
　shame,
　With all its grace, is given;
Their name an everlasting name,
　Their joy the joy of heaven.

They suffer with their Lord below,
They reign with Him above,
Their profit and their joy to know
The mystery of His love.

Sunday after Ascension Day.

Hymn 136.   III.   TEN COMMANDMENTS.

O LORD, how little do we know,
  How little of Thy presence feel,
While we continue here below,
  And in these earthly temples dwell.

When will these veils of flesh remove,
  And not eclipse the sight of God?
When wilt Thou take us up above
  To see Thy face without a cloud?

Dart in our hearts a heavenly ray,
  A ray which still may shine more bright,
Increasing to the perfect day,
  Till we awake in endless light.

Then shall each star become a sun,
  Filled with a lustre all divine:
Each shall possess a radiant crown,
  And to eternal ages shine.

Sunday after Ascension Day.

mn 137. IV. CULBACH.

ALWAYS with us, always with us,
  Words of cheer and words of love;
Thus the risen Saviour whispers
  From His dwelling-place above.

With us when we toil in sadness,
  Sowing much, and reaping none,
Telling us that in the future
  Golden harvests may be won.

With us when the storm is sweeping
  O'er our pathway dark and drear:
Waking hope within our bosoms,
  Stifling every anxious fear.

With us in the lonely valley,
  When we cross the chilling stream,
Lighting up the steps to glory
  With Salvation's radiant beam.

Whit Sunday.

Hymn 138.

TALLIS'S VENI CREATOR.

SAVIOUR, Thy Father's promise send :
Spirit of holiness, descend :
Lo, we are waiting for Thee, Lord,
All in one place with one accord.

Come and convince us all of sin,
Lighting Thy lamp our hearts within ;
Thy temples, but alas, how slow
Thy presence and Thy voice to know.

Convince us all of righteousness :—
By that great work Thy people bless,
Which our High Priest hath wrought alone,
And carried to His Father's throne.

Of judgment, Lord, convince us too :
Teach us in Christ all things to view :
O make us pure, with lightened eyes,
Harmless as doves, as serpents wise.

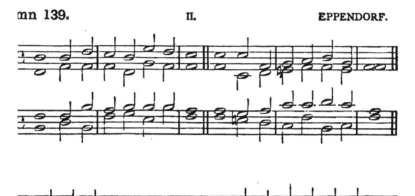

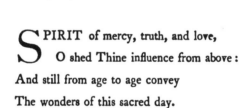

S PIRIT of mercy, truth, and love,
    O shed Thine influence from above :
And still from age to age convey
The wonders of this sacred day.

In every clime, by every tongue,
Be God's surpassing glory sung ;
Let all the listening earth be taught
The wonders by our Saviour wrought.

Unfailing Comfort, heavenly Guide,
Still o'er Thy holy Church preside :
Still let mankind Thy blessings prove,
Spirit of mercy, truth, and love.

Whit Sunday.

Hymn 140. III. ANGELS' SONG.

CREATOR Spirit, by whose aid
The world's foundations first were laid,
Come visit every pious mind,
Come pour Thy joys on human kind:
From sin and sorrow set us free,
And make Thy temples worthy Thee.

O source of uncreated light,
The Father's promised Paraclete;
Thrice holy Fount, thrice holy Fire,
Our hearts with heavenly love inspire:
Come, and Thy sacred unction bring,
To sanctify us while we sing.

Plenteous of grace descend from high,
Rich in Thy sevenfold energy,
Make us eternal truth receive,
And practise all that we believe:
Give us Thyself, that we may see
The Father and the Son by Thee.

Immortal honour, endless fame,
Attend the Almighty Father's Name:
The Saviour Son be glorified,
Who for lost man's redemption died:
And equal adoration be,
Eternal Paraclete, to Thee.

Whit Sunday.

Hymn 141. IV. WHEATFIELD.

SOURCE of good, whose power controls
    Every movement of our souls;
Wind that quickens where it blows;
Comforter of human woes;
Lamp of God, whose ray serene
In the darkest night is seen;
Come, inspire my feeble strain,
That I may not sing in vain.

God's own finger, skilled to teach
Tongues of every land and speech;
Balsam of the wounded soul,
Binding up, and making whole;
Flame of pure and holy love;
Strength of all that live and move;
Come, Thy gifts and fire impart;
Make me love Thee from the heart.

As the hart, with longing, looks
For refreshing water-brooks,
Heated in the burning chase;
So my soul desires Thy grace;
So my heavy-laden breast,
By the cares of life opprest,
Longs Thy cooling streams to taste,
In this dry and barren waste.

Hymn 142. VIENI

G RACIOUS Spirit, Love divine,
Let Thy light around us shine :
All our guilty fears remove ;
Fill us with Thy peace and love.

Pardon to the contrite give,
Bid the wounded sinner live ;
Lead us to the Lamb of God,
Wash us in His precious blood.

Earnest Thou of heavenly rest,
Comfort every troubled breast ;
Life, and joy, and peace impart,
Sanctifying every heart.

Guardian Spirit, lest we stray,
Keep us in the heavenly way :
Bring us to Thy courts above,
Realms of light and endless love.

Hymn 143.

WAREHAM.

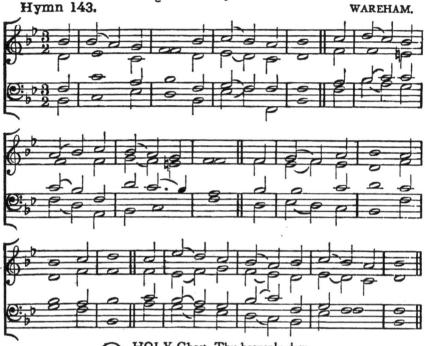

O HOLY Ghost, Thy heavenly dew
    The hearts of sinners can renew;
Thou dost within our hearts abide,
And still to holy action guide.

Thou mak'st the soul with joy to sing
When sorrow's clouds are deepening:
With Jesus Christ Thou mak'st us one,
Earnest of heaven from God's high throne.

Best gift of God, and man's true Friend,
Into my inmost soul descend:
The mind of Jesus Christ impart,
And consecrate to Thee my heart.

Teach me to do my Father's will,
To lie beneath His guidance still;
Lighten my mind, and O incline
My heart to make His pleasure mine.

From spot and blemish make me pure,
My future bliss in heaven secure:
When lost in darkness give me light,
And cheer me through death's dreary night.

Trinity Sunday.

Hymn 144.

* *In certain lines of the 2nd, 3rd, and 4th verses the minims thus marked ♩ must be divided into two crotchets, and the dotted slurs disregarded.*

HOLY, Holy, Holy, Lord God Almighty!
Early in the morning our song shall rise to Thee,
Holy, Holy, Holy! Merciful and Mighty!
God in Three Persons, blessed Trinity.

Holy, Holy, Holy! All the saints adore Thee,.
Casting down their golden crowns around the glassy sea;
Cherubim and Seraphim falling down before Thee,
Which wast, and art, and evermore shalt be!

Holy, Holy, Holy! Though the darkness hide Thee,
Though the eye of sinful man Thy glory may not see,
Only Thou art Holy, there is none beside Thee,
Perfect in power, in love, and purity!

Holy, Holy, Holy, Lord God Almighty!
All Thy works shall praise Thy name, in earth, and sky, and sea;
Holy, Holy, Holy! Merciful and Mighty!
God in Three Persons, blessed Trinity!

Trinity Sunday.

W E give immortal praise
　　To God the Father's love,
For all our comforts here,
　　And better hopes above :
He sent His own eternal Son
To die for sins that man had done.

To God the Son belongs
　　Immortal glory too,
Who bought us with His blood
　　From everlasting woe :
And now He lives, and now He reigns,
And sees the fruit of all His pains.

To God the Spirit's name
　　Immortal worship give,
Whose new creating power
　　Makes the dead sinner live :
His work completes the great design,
And fills the soul with joy divine.

Almighty God, to Thee
　　Be endless honour done,
The undivided Three,
　　And the mysterious One.
Where reason fails with all her powers,
There faith prevails and love adores.

Trinity Sunday.

FATHER of heaven, whose love profound
A ransom for our souls hath found,
Before Thy throne we sinners bend ;
To us Thy pardoning love extend.

Almighty Son, incarnate Word,
Our Prophet, Priest, Redeemer, Lord ;
Before Thy throne we sinners bend ;
To us Thy saving grace extend.

Eternal Spirit, by whose breath
The soul is raised from sin and death,
Before Thy throne we sinners bend ;
To us Thy quickening power extend.

Jehovah, Father, Spirit, Son,
Mysterious Godhead, Three in One,
Before Thy throne we sinners bend ;
Grace, pardon, life, to us extend.

Trinity Sunday.

Hymn 147.   IV.   HAMBURGH.

HOLY, holy, holy Lord,
    God of Hosts! when heaven and earth
Out of darkness, at Thy word,
  Issued into glorious birth,
All Thy works before Thee stood,
And Thine eye beheld them good,
While they sang with one accord,
Holy, holy, holy Lord !

Holy, holy, holy ! Thee
  One Jehovah, evermore
Father, Son, and Spirit, we,
  Dust and ashes, would adore :
Lightly by the world esteemed,
From that world by Thee redeemed,
Sing we here, with glad accord,
Holy, holy, holy Lord !

Holy, holy, holy! all
  Heaven's triumphant choir shall sing,
When the ransomed nations fall
  At the footstool of their King.
Then shall Saints and Seraphim,
Hearts and voices, swell one hymn,
Round the throne with one accord,
Holy, holy, holy Lord !

First Sunday after Trinity.

Hymn 148. I. RATISBON.

SINCE we kept the Saviour's birth,
  Half the yearly course is flown;
We have followed Him on earth,
  We have tracked Him to His throne:
    Grateful now we stand, and greet
    Our salvation wrought complete.

What one sweetest flower and best
  Decks the Garden of the Spouse?
What one gem beyond the rest
  Sparkles on the Victor's brows?
    What one strain in heaven above
    Swells the chorus? GOD IS LOVE.

Thou who lovedst us on high,
  Looking from the seats of bliss,
Then, to take our misery,
  Passedst through a world like this,
    Of Thy Spirit, Lord, impart,
    Warm with love each grateful heart.

To the brethren evermore,
  To the neighbour dwelling by,
To the outcast at our door,
  To the needy when they cry,
    Grant us each in love to be
    As Thy Church hath learned of Thee.

First Sunday after Trinity.

Hymn 149.　　　　　　　　H.　　　　　　　　LEIPSIC.

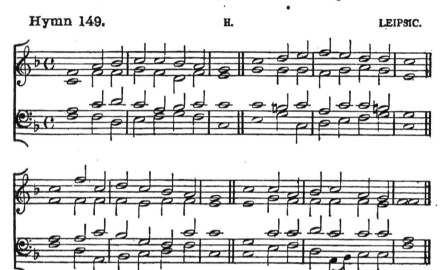

O THOU, who camest from above,
　The pure, celestial fire to impart,
Kindle a flame of sacred love
　On the mean altar of my heart.

There let it for Thy glory burn
　With inextinguishable blaze;
And, trembling, to its source return,
　In humble prayer and fervent praise.

Jesus! confirm my heart's desire
　To work, and speak, and think for Thee;
Still let me guard the holy fire,
　And still stir up Thy gift in me:

Ready for all Thy perfect will,
　My acts of faith and love repeat;
Till death Thy endless mercies seal,
　And make my sacrifice complete.

Hymn 150. III. ST. JAMES.

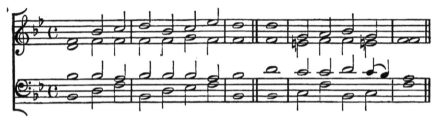

C OME, let us join our cheerful songs
    With angels round the throne;
Ten thousand thousand are their tongues,
    But all their joys are one.

" Worthy the Lamb that died," they cry,
    To be exalted thus :
" Worthy the Lamb," our lips reply,
    For He was slain for us.

Lord, Thou art worthy to receive
    Honour and power divine ;
And blessings, more than we can give,
    For evermore be Thine.

Let all creation join in one
    To bless the sacred name
Of Him who sits upon the throne,
    And to adore the Lamb.

G O, worship at Immanuel's feet;
    See, in His face what wonders meet:
Earth is too narrow to express
His worth, His glory, or His grace.

Is He compared to Wine or Bread?
Dear Lord, our souls would thus be fed:
That Flesh, that dying Blood of Thine,
Is Bread of Life, is heavenly Wine.

Is He a Door? I'll enter in;
Behold the pastures large and green!
A paradise divinely fair;
None but the sheep have freedom there.

Is He a Temple? I adore
The indwelling majesty and power;
And still to His most Holy Place,
Whene'er I pray, I turn my face.

Nor earth, nor seas, nor sun, nor stars,
Nor heaven His full remembrance bears;
His beauties we can never trace,
Till we behold Him face to face.

Second Sunday after Trinity.

Hymn 152.

NASSAU.

LO, the feast is spread to-day,
Jesus summons, come away !
From the vanity of life,
From the sounds of mirth or strife,
To the feast by Jesus given,
Come, and taste the Bread of Heaven.

Why, with proud excuse and vain,
Spurn His mercy once again ?
From amidst life's social ties,
From the farm and merchandise,
Come, for all is now prepared :
Freely given, be freely shared.

Blessed are the lips that taste
Our Redeemer's marriage-feast;
Blessed, who on Him shall feed,
Bread of Life, and drink indeed ;
Blessed, for their thirst is o'er;
They shall never hunger more.

Make then once again your choice,
Hear to-day His calling voice :
Servants, do your Master's will ;
Bidden guests, His table fill ;
Come, before His wrath shall swear
Ye shall never enter there.

Second Sunday after Trinity.

Hymn 153. II. DIX.

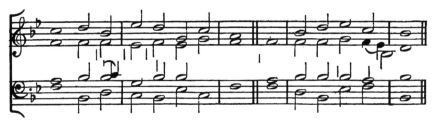

G OOD and pleasant 'tis to see
    Brethren dwell in unity,
When the law which Jesus taught
Rules each word, and deed, and thought.

God has promised there, we know,
Blessings richly to bestow,
Life on earth with all its store,
Life in heaven for evermore.

Jesu, Head of Christians all,
Grant that we, both great and small,
Through Thy Gospel's light divine,
May be one and wholly Thine.

Bring back all that go astray,
Heavenly Shepherd, to Thy way:
'Neath Thy favour and Thy light
All Thy pasture-sheep unite.

Bind together heart and heart,
Let no strife the union part:
With Thine own Almighty hand
Knit the sacred brother-band.

Let this band of brothers love
Here on earth, in heaven above:
Love, and praise, and rest in Thee,
Here, and through eternity.

Second Sunday after Trinity.

JESU! the very thought of Thee
　　With sweetness fills the breast:
But sweeter far Thy face to see,
　　And in Thy presence rest.

No voice can sing, no heart can frame,
　　Nor can the memory find
A sweeter sound than Jesu's Name,
　　The Saviour of mankind.

O hope of every contrite heart,
　　O joy of all the meek,
To those who fall how kind Thou art!
　　How good to those who seek!

But what to those who find? Ah, this
　　No tongue nor pen can shew:
The love of Jesus, what it is,
　　None but His loved ones know.

Jesu! our only joy we know,
　　As Thou our prize wilt be;
In Thee be all our glory now,
　　And through eternity.

Second Sunday after Trinity.

Hymn 155.   IV.   MUNDEN.

WHO are these, like stars appearing,
　　These, before God's throne who stand ?
Each a golden crown is wearing,
　Who are all this glorious band ?
　　Hallelujah! hark, they sing,
　　Praising loud their heavenly King.

Who are these in dazzling brightness,
　Clothed in God's own righteousness ;
These, whose robes of purest whiteness
　Shall their lustre still possess ;
　　Still untouched by time's rude hand ;
　　Whence come all this glorious band ?

These are they who have contended
　For their Saviour's honour long,
Wrestling on till life was ended,
　Following not the sinful throng :
　　These, who well the fight sustained,
　　Victory through the Lamb have gained.

These are they whose hearts were riven,
　Sore with woe and anguish tried,
Who in prayer full oft have striven
　With the God they magnified :
　　Now their painful conflict's o'er
　　God has bid them weep no more.

Third Sunday after Trinity.

HARK, through the courts of heaven
   Voices of angels sound ;
" He that was dead now lives again ;
   He that was lost is found."

God of unfailing grace,
   Send down thy Spirit now ;
Raise the dejected soul to hope,
   And make the lofty bow.

In countries far from home,
   On earthly husks we feed ;
Back to our Father's house, O Lord,
   Our wandering footsteps lead.

Then at each soul's return
   The heavenly harps shall sound,
" He that was dead now lives again ;
   He that was lost is found."

Third Sunday after Trinity.

RETURN, O wanderer, to thy home:
   Thy Father calls for thee :
No longer now an exile roam,
   In guilt and misery.

Return, O wanderer, to thy home:
   'Tis Jesus calls for thee :
The Spirit and the Bride say, Come ;
   O now for refuge flee !

Return, O wanderer, to thy home :
   'Tis madness to delay ;
There are no pardons in the tomb,
   And brief is mercy's day.

Third Sunday after Trinity.

Hymn 158.   III.   CEYLON.

" SPEAK, for Thy servant heareth,"—
    Thus give us grace, O Lord,
To listen and to answer
    Whene'er Thy voice is heard:
Whether we wait expectant
    Its sound to guide us home;
Or all unsought, unwelcome,
    Its sudden warning come.

Above the whirl of traffic,
    Above the stir of life,
Amidst the songs of pleasure,
    And o'er the din of strife,
May never cease within us
    Thy whispers soft and clear,
Nor ready hearts, replying,
    " Speak, Lord, Thy servants hear."

And in the latest conflict,
    When strength and faith are low,
And all our schemes of comfort
    Are baffled by the foe:
Amid life's feeble throbbings,
    Yet nearer and more near
May Thy sweet tones of solace
    Speak, and Thy servants hear.

Third Sunday after Trinity.

Hymn 159.   IV.   CHARA.

* In the first verse, this bar and the following must be performed thus :—

and in the 2nd verse thus :—

THERE was joy in heaven,
There was joy in heaven,
When, this goodly world to frame,
The Lord of might and mercy came ;
Shouts of joy were heard on high,
And the stars sang from the sky,
"Glory to God in heaven !"

There was joy in heaven,
There was joy in heaven,
When of love the midnight beam
Dawned on the towers of Bethlehem :
And along the echoing hill,
Angels sang, "On earth goodwill,
And glory in the heaven !"

There is joy in heaven,
There is joy in heaven,
When the sheep that went astray
Turns again to Zion's way :
When the soul, by grace subdued,
Sobs its prayer of gratitude,—
Then there is joy in heaven.

Fourth Sunday after Trinity.

Hymn 160.　　　　　　　　　I.　　　　　　MECKLENBURGH.

SEE the ransomed millions stand,
　　Palms of conquest in their hand ;
This before the Throne their strain :
" Hell is vanquish'd ; Death is slain ;
Blessing, honour, glory, might,
Are the Conqueror's native right ;
Thrones and powers before Him fall ;
Lamb of God, and Lord of all !"

Hasten, Lord, the promised hour ;
Come in glory and in power ;
Still Thy foes are unsubdued ;
Nature sighs to be renewed ;
Time has nearly reached its sum,
All things with Thy Bride say, "Come ;"
Jesus, whom all worlds adore,
Come, and reign for evermore !

Fourth Sunday after Trinity.

Hymn 161.   II.   ABBEY.

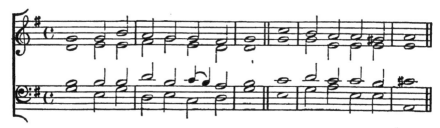

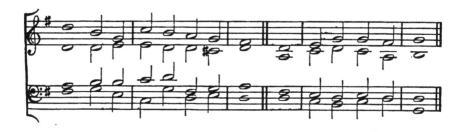

LIGHT of the lonely pilgrim's heart,
 Star of the coming day !
Arise, and with Thy morning beams
 Chase all our griefs away !

Come, blessed Lord ! let every shore
 And answering island sing
The praises of Thy Royal Name,
 And own Thee as their King.

Bid the whole earth, responsive now
 To the bright world above,
Break forth in sweetest strains of joy
 In memory of Thy love.

Jesus ! Thy fair creation groans,
 The air, the earth, the sea,
In unison with all our hearts,
 And calls aloud for Thee.

Thine was the Cross, with all its fruits
 Of grace and peace divine :
Be Thine the crown of glory now,
 The palm of victory Thine !

Fourth Sunday after Trinity.

Hymn 162.   III.   TROYTE.

MY God and Father, while' I stray,
  Far from my home, on life's'
rough way,
O teach me from my heart' to say,
  Thy will' be done!

Though dark my path and sad' my lot,
Let me be still and mur'mur not,
Or breathe the prayer divine'ly taught,
  Thy will' be done!

What though in lonely grief' I sigh,
For friends beloved, no lon'ger nigh,
Submissive still would I' reply,
  Thy will' be done!

Though Thou hast called me to' resign
What most I prized, it ne'er' was mine,
I have but yielded what' was Thine;
  Thy will' be done!

Should grief or sickness waste' away,
My life in premature' decay,
My Father! still I strive' to say,
  Thy will' be done!

Let but my fainting heart' be blest
With Thy sweet Spirit for' its guest,
My God, to Thee I leave' the rest;
  Thy will' be done!

Renew my will from day' to day;
Blend it with Thine, and take' away
All that now makes it hard' to say,
  Thy will' be done!

Then, when on earth I breathe' no more,
The prayer, oft mixed with tears' before,
I'll sing upon a hap'pier shore,
  Thy will' be done!

Fourth Sunday after Trinity.

I LOVE Thy kingdom, Lord,
 The house of Thine abode,
The Church our blest Redeemer saved
 With His own precious blood.

I love Thy Church, O God,
 Her walls before Thee stand,
Dear as the apple of Thine eye,
 And graven on Thy hand.

Beyond my highest joy,
 I prize her heavenly ways,
Her sweet communion, solemn vows,
 Her hymns of love and praise.

Jesus, Thou Friend divine,
 Our Saviour and our King,
Thy hand from every snare and foe
 Shall great deliverance bring.

Sure as Thy truth shall last,
 To Zion shall be given
The brightest glories earth shall yield,
 And brighter bliss of heaven.

Fifth Sunday after Trinity.

Hymn 164.   *Fourple* I.   TYTHERTON.

O GOD, for ever near !
    We humbly will rejoice,
For well we know that Thou art here,
    And listening to our voice.

    Up to Thy mercy-seat
    'Tis good for us to go :
For there Thou dost Thy people meet,
    Rich blessings to bestow.

    And now, no longer veiled,
    The mercy-seat is free :
The great High-Priest for man prevailed,
    To clear our way to Thee.

    We praise Thee as we bend,
    And here Thy praise forth tell,
Because Thy love doth condescend
    Within this house to dwell.

Fifth Sunday after Trinity.

Hymn 165.   II.   JERSEY.

J ESUS, Lord, we look to Thee,
  Let us in Thy Name agree ;
Shew Thyself the Prince of Peace,
Bid all strife for ever cease.

Make us of one heart and mind,
Courteous, pitiful, and kind :
Lowly, meek, in thought and word,
Altogether like our Lord.

Let us for each other care,
Each the other's burden bear,
To Thy Church the pattern give,
Shew how true believers live.

Free from anger and from pride,
Let us thus in God abide :
All the depths of love express,
All the heights of holiness.

Fifth Sunday after Trinity.

Hymn 166.   III.   WARFARE.

Unis.

MUCH in sorrow, oft in woe,
  Onward, Christians, onward go ;
Fight the fight, and worn with strife,
Steep with tears the Bread of Life.
Onward, Christians, onward go :
Join the war and face the foe :
Faint not ! much doth yet remain
Dreary is the long campaign.

Shrink not, Christians ! will ye yield ?
Will ye quit the painful field ?
Will ye flee in danger's hour ?
Know ye not your Captain's power ?
Let your drooping hearts be glad :
March, in heavenly armour clad :
Fight, nor think the battle long :
Victory soon shall tune your song.

Let not sorrow dim your eye,
Soon shall every tear be dry :
Let not woe your course impede :
Great your strength, if great your need.
Onward then to battle move ;
More than conquerors ye shall prove ;
Though opposed by many a foe,
Christian soldiers, onward go.

Fifth Sunday after Trinity.

Hymn 167.   IV.   CASSELL.

"ALL the night and nothing taken,"—
    How shall we let down the net?
All our steadfast hopes are shaken,
    Every scheme with failure met:
      Though we speak the message clear,
      Yet the sinner will not hear.

"All the night, and nothing taken,"—
    And the hours are speeding by;
Is the chosen flock forsaken?
    Is no Master standing nigh?
      Nought is found among the band
      But faint heart, and weary hand.

Still, though night may pass in sorrow,
    And no guiding star appear,
Sounds the promise for the morrow
    From the Master standing near:
      "Ye shall find"—then hopeful yet
      At His word we loose the net.

Sixth Sunday after Trinity.

Hymn 168.

CRÜGER.

L ORD, when before Thy throne we meet,
        Thy goodness to adore,
From heaven, the eternal mercy-seat,
    On us Thy blessing pour,
And make our inmost souls to be
An habitation meet for Thee.

The Body for our ransom given ;
    The Blood in mercy shed ;
With this immortal food from heaven,
    Lord, let our souls be fed :
And, as we round Thy table kneel,
Help us Thy quickening grace to feel.

Be Thou, O Holy Spirit, nigh :
    Accept the humble prayer,
The contrite soul's repentant sigh,
    The sinner's heartfelt tear :
And let our adoration rise,
As fragrant incense, to the skies.

Sixth Sunday after Trinity.

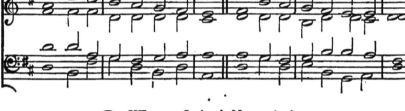

O YE, your Saviour's Name who bear,
   Who know the truth His words declare,
Are bought with His most precious blood,
Buried in His baptismal flood ;—

Bear not the name of Christ alone,
If ye would reach His glorious throne;
O never from His laws depart,
But Christians be in life and heart.

He who would reign with Christ above,
Must here, in faith and patient love,
First tread that rough and thorny road
Which Christ before him meekly trod.

He who his Saviour rightly knows,
And on his way devoutly goes,
When life is o'er shall sweetly rest,
And be with God for ever blest.

Hymn 170.   III.   QUAM DILECTA.

W E love the place, O Lord,
   Wherein Thine honour dwells,
The joy of Thy abode
   All other joy excels.

We love the house of prayer,
   Wherein Thy servants meet :
For Thou, O Lord, art there,
   Thy chosen ones to greet.

We love Thy saints who come
   Thy mercy to proclaim,
To call the wanderers home,
   And magnify Thy Name.

Our first and latest love
   To Zion shall be given,
The House of God above,
   On earth the gate of heaven.

Sixth Sunday after Trinity.

HEAVENLY Father, to whose eye
　　Future things unfolded lie,
Through the desert, where I stray,
Let Thy counsel guide my way.

Lord, uphold me day by day:
Shed a light upon my way:
Guide me through perplexing snares:
Care for me in all my cares.

All I ask for is, enough:
Only, when the way is rough,
Let Thy rod and staff impart
Strength and courage to my heart.

Should Thy wisdom, Lord, decree
Trials long and sharp for me,
Pain or sorrow, care or shame,—
Father, glorify Thy Name.

Let me neither faint nor fear,
Feeling still that Thou art near,
In the course my Saviour trod,
Tending still to Thee, my God.

Seventh Sunday after Trinity.

Hymn 172.   I.   GOUDIMEL.

B READ of the world, in mercy broken,
  Wine of the soul, in mercy shed,
By whom the words of life were spoken,
    And in whose death our sins are dead,—
Look on the heart by sorrow broken,
    Look on the tears by sinners shed,
And be Thy feast to us the token
    That by Thy grace our souls are fed.

Seventh Sunday after Trinity.

TO God the only wise,
　　Our Saviour and our King,
Let all the saints below the skies
　Their humble praises bring.

'Tis His Almighty love,
　His counsel and His care,
Preserves us safe from sin and death,
　And every hurtful snare.

He will present our souls,
　Unblemished and complete,
Before the glory of His face,
　With joys divinely great.

Then all the chosen seed
　Shall meet before the throne,
Shall bless the conduct of His grace,
　And make His wonders known.

To our Redeemer God
Wisdom and power belongs,
Immortal crowns of majesty,
And never-ending songs.

Hymn 174.   III.   HYMNUS EUCHARISTICUS.

B OWED with the guilt of sin, O God,
    Expectant of the chastening rod,
O may, whate'er Thy will decree,
Our suffering come alone from Thee!

Then need we fear, with Thee for judge,
No wild caprice, no rankling grudge :
Wrath calmed by love is Thine alone :
Thy majesty and mercy, one.

O prayer of little faith and trust !
What is the arm of man but dust ?
The wrath of foes shall seethe in vain,
If Thou the lifted arm restrain.

Yet, as the child may shrink with fright
Lest any but the father smite,
We in our weakness none would see
Between Thy suffering ones and Thee.

And thus, as prayed, with shame low-bent,
Of old that Royal Penitent,
Into Thy hands, Lord, let us fall :
In wrath or mercy, be Thou all !

Seventh Sunday after Trinity.

Hymn 175.   IV.   MELCOMBE.

JESUS, thou Joy of loving hearts,
    Thou Fount of Life, Thou Light
        of men !
From the best bliss that earth imparts,
    We turn unfilled to Thee again.

Thy truth unchanged hath ever stood ;
    Thou savest those that on Thee call ;
To them that seek Thee, Thou art good,
    To them that find Thee, All in All.

We taste Thee, O Thou living Bread,
    And long to feast upon Thee still :
We drink of Thee, the Fountain Head,
    And thirst our souls from Thee to fill.

Our restless spirits yearn for Thee,
    Where'er our changeful lot is cast ;
Glad, when Thy gracious smile we see,
    Blest, when our faith can hold Thee fast.

O Jesus, ever with us stay !
    Make all our moments calm and bright :
Chase the dark night of sin away,
    Shed o'er the world Thy holy light !

Eighth Sunday after Trinity.

THE Spirit, in our hearts,
  Is whispering, "Sinner, come : "
The Bride, the Church of Christ, proclaims
  To all His children, " Come ! "

Let him that heareth say,
  To all about him, " Come ! "
Let him that thirsts for righteousness,
  To Christ, the Fountain, come !

Yea, whosoever will,
  O let him freely come,
And freely drink the stream of life
  'Tis Jesus bids him come.

Lo, Jesus, who invites,
  Declares, " I quickly come ; "
" Lord, even so ! " we wait Thine hour,
  O blest Redeemer, come !

Eighth Sunday after Trinity.

I N memory of the Saviour's love
　　We keep the sacred feast,
Where every humble contrite heart
　　Is made a welcome guest.

By faith we take the Bread of Life,
　　With which our souls are fed ;
And Cup, in token of His Blood
　　That was for sinners shed.

Under His banner thus we sing
　　The wonders of His love,
And thus anticipate by faith
　　The heavenly feast above.

Eighth Sunday after Trinity.

Hymn 178. III. NOTTINGHAM.

PRAYER is the Christian's vital breath,
 The Christian's native air :
His watchword at the gates of death :
 He enters heaven with prayer.

The saints, in prayer, appear as one,
 In word, and deed, and mind,
While with the Father and the Son
 Sweet fellowship they find.

Nor prayer is made by man alone :
 The Holy Spirit pleads ;
And Jesus, on the Eternal Throne,
 For sinners intercedes.

O Thou, by whom we come to God !
 The Life, the Truth, the Way !
The path of prayer Thyself hast trod :
 Lord, teach us how to pray.

Eighth Sunday after Trinity.

Hymn 179.   IV.   VULPIUS.

MIGHTY Saviour, gracious King,
   Now Thy waiting people bless;
Thou that dost deliverance bring,
   Come to reign in righteousness.
Thou dost heavenly light impart;
   Tune the ear to Zion's song;
Teach and guide the wayward heart,
   Loose and prompt the stammering tongue.

Pour Thy Spirit from on high;
   Come, Thy mourning Church to bless;
Streams of life and joy supply;
   Fill the world with righteousness;
Light shall then possess Thine own,
   Holy quiet, perfect peace;
And where heavenly seed is sown,
   Thou wilt give the blest increase.

Ninth Sunday after Trinity.

Hymn 180.

GIBBONS'S ST. MATTHIAS.

O FATHER of long-suffering grace,
   Thou who hast sworn to stay
Pleading with sinners face to face
   Through all their devious way :

Too oft, within this camp of Thine,
   Rebellious murmurs rise :
Sin cannot bear to see Thee shine
   So awful to her eyes.

Fain would our lawless hearts escape
   And with the heathen be,
To worship every monstrous shape
   In fancied darkness free.

Vain thought, that shall not be at all—
   Refuse we or obey,
Our ears have heard the Almighty's call,
   We cannot be as they.

Lord, wave again Thy chastening rod,
   Till every idol throne
Crumble to dust, and Thou, O God,
   Reign in our hearts alone.

Ninth Sunday after Trinity.

Hymn 181.   II.   ST. STEPHEN'S.

FORTH to the land of promise bound,
 Our desert path we tread;
God's fiery pillar for our guide,
 His Captain at our head.

E'en now we faintly trace the hills,
 And catch their distant blue;
And the bright city's gleaming spires
 Rise dimly on our view.

Soon, when the desert shall be crossed,
 The flood of death past o'er,
Our pilgrim hosts shall safely land
 On Canaan's peaceful shore.

There love shall have its perfect work,
 And prayer be lost in praise;
And all the servants of our God
 Their endless anthem raise.

Q 2

Ninth Sunday after Trinity.

Hymn 182.　　　　　　　　　**III.**　　　　　　　　　**ST. MATTHIAS.**

CAPTAIN of Israel's host, and Guide
　　Of all who seek their home above :
Beneath Thy shadow we abide,
　The cloud of Thy protecting love :
Our strength, Thy grace : our rule, Thy word :
Our end, the glory of the Lord.

By Thine unerring Spirit led,
　We shall not in the desert stray :
By Thy paternal bounty fed,
　We shall not lack in all our way :
As far from danger as from fear,
While Thine Almighty Love is near.

Ninth Sunday after Trinity.

Hymn 183.　　　　　　　IV.　　　　　　CHESTER-GATE.

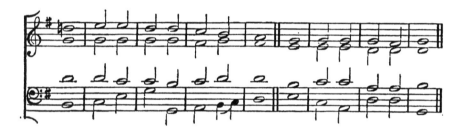

O HOLY Saviour, Friend unseen,
　The faint, the weak, on Thee
　　may lean;
Help me, throughout life's varying scene,
　By faith to cling to Thee!

Blest with communion so divine,
Take what Thou wilt, shall I repine,
When, as the branches to the vine,
　My soul may cling to Thee?

Though faith and hope awhile be tried,
I ask not, need not, aught beside;
How safe, how calm, how satisfied,
　The souls that cling to Thee!

They fear not life's rough storms to brave,
Since Thou art near, and strong to save:
Nor shudder e'en at death's dark wave,
　Because they cling to Thee.

Blest is my lot, whate'er befall:
What can disturb me, who appal,
While, as my Strength, my Rock, my All,
　Saviour, I cling to Thee!

Tenth Sunday after Trinity.

Hymn 184.

ST. BRIDE.

DID Christ o'er sinners weep,
  And shall our cheeks be dry?
Let floods of penitential grief
  Burst forth from every eye.

The Son of God in tears
  The angels wondering see:
Hast thou no wonder, O my soul?
  He shed those tears for thee.

He wept that we might weep,
  Might weep our sin and shame;
He wept to shew His love to us,
  And bid us love the same.

Then tender be our hearts,
  Our eyes in sorrow dim,
Till every tear from every eye
  Is wiped away by Him.

Tenth Sunday after Trinity.

mn 185.   II.   LUDLOW.

COME, Holy Spirit, come;
   Let Thy bright beams arise;
Dispel the sorrow from our minds,
   The darkness from our eyes.

Convince us of our sin,
   And lead us to the Lord;
And to our wondering view reveal
   The mercies of Thy Word.

Revive our drooping faith,
   Our doubts and fears remove:
And kindle in our hearts the flame
   Of everlasting love.

To God the Father, Son,
   And Spirit, glory be:
As was, and is, and shall be so
   To all eternity.

Tenth Sunday after Trinity.

Hymn 186.　　　　　　　　III.　　　　　　　　LONGHURST.

O THOU, the contrite sinners' Friend,
　Who, loving, lov'st them to the end,
On this alone my hopes depend,
　That Thou wilt plead for me.

When, weary in the Christian race,
Far off appears my resting-place,
And fainting I mistrust Thy grace,
　Then, Saviour, plead for me.

When I have erred and gone astray,
Afar from Thine and wisdom's way,
And see no glimmering guiding ray,
　Still, Saviour, plead for me.

When Satan, by my sins made bold,
Strives from Thy Cross to loose my hold,
Then with Thy pitying arms enfold,
　And plead, O plead for me !

And when my dying hour draws near,
Darkened with anguish, guilt, and fear,
Then to my fainting sight appear,
　Pleading in heaven for me.

Tenth Sunday after Trinity.

Hymn 187.   IV.   REINAGLE.

H OW honourable is the place
    Where we adoring stand,
Zion, the glory of the earth,
    And beauty of the land.

Bulwarks of mighty grace defend
    The city where we dwell;
The walls, of strong salvation made,
    Defy the assaults of hell.

Lift up the everlasting gates,
    The doors wide open fling;
Enter, ye nations, that obey
    The statutes of our King.

Here shall we taste eternal joys,
    And live in perfect peace;
We that have known Jehovah's name,
    And ventured on His grace.

Eleventh Sunday after Trinity.

MARTYRS'.

L ORD, like the publican I stand,
　And lift my heart to Thee ;
Thy pardoning grace, O God, command ;
　Be merciful to me.

I smite upon my anxious breast,
　O'erwhelmed with agony !
O save my soul by sin oppressed ;
　Be merciful to me.

My guilt, my shame, I all confess,
　I have no hope nor plea
But Jesus' blood and righteousness :
　Be merciful to me.

Here at Thy Cross I still would wait,
　Nor from its shelter flee,
Till Thou, O God, in mercy great,
　Art merciful to me.

Eleventh Sunday after Trinity.

O GOD, unseen, yet ever near,
  Thy presence may we feel;
And thus, inspired with holy fear,
  Before Thine altar kneel.

Here may Thy faithful people know
  The blessings of Thy love;
The streams that through the desert flow;
  The manna from above.

We come, obedient to Thy word,
  To feast on heavenly food;
Our meat, the Body of the Lord;
  Our drink, His precious Blood.

Thus may we all Thy words obey;
  For we, O God, are Thine;
And go rejoicing on our way,
  Renewed with strength divine.

Eleventh Sunday after Trinity.

Hymn 190.   III.   WINDSOR.

O THOU, from whom all goodness
    flows,
  I lift my soul to Thee:
In all my sorrows, conflicts, woes,
  Good Lord, remember me.

When on my aching burdened heart
  My sins lie heavily,
My pardon speak, new peace impart,
  Good Lord, remember me.

If on my face for Thy dear Name,
  Shame and reproaches be,
All hail reproach and welcome shame,
  If Thou remember me.

If worn with pain, disease and grief,
  This feeble frame should be,
Grant patience, rest, and kind relief:
  Hear, and remember me.

When, in the solemn hour of death,
  I wait Thy just decree,
Saviour, with my last parting breath
  I'll cry, Remember me.

Eleventh Sunday after Trinity.

TO me a sinner, chief' of all,
   O God, be merciful !
Though guilt for judgment on' me call,
   My God, be merciful !

O Father, from whose house' I strayed,
   To me be merciful !
O Christ, on whom my sins' were laid,
   Do Thou be merciful !

O Spirit, pleading oft' in vain,
   Thou, too, be merciful !
Depart not from me, but' remain,
   With patience merciful.

O Father, Son, and Ho'ly Ghost,
   One God, be merciful !
To me, of sinners sin'ning most,
   O God, be merciful !

Twelfth Sunday after Trinity.

Hymn 192.

COLMAR.

WE saw Thee not when Thou didst come
    To this poor world of sin and death,
Nor e'er beheld Thy cottage home
    In that despised Nazareth:
But we believe Thy footsteps trod
Its streets and plains, Thou Son of God.

We did not see Thee lifted high
    Amid that wild and savage crew,
Nor heard thy meek, imploring cry,
    " Forgive, they know not what they do:"
Yet we believe the deed was done
Which shook the earth, and veiled the sun.

We stood not by the empty tomb
    Where late Thy sacred body lay,
Nor sat within that upper room,
    Nor met Thee in the open way:
But we believe that angels said,
" Why seek the living with the dead?"

We did not mark the chosen few,
    When Thou didst through the clouds ascend,
First lift to heaven their wondering view,
    Then to the earth all prostrate bend:
Yet we believe that mortal eyes
Beheld that journey to the skies.

And now that Thou dost reign on high,
    And thence Thy waiting people bless,
No ray of glory from the sky
    Doth shine upon our wilderness:
But we believe Thy faithful Word,
And trust in our redeeming Lord.

Twelfth Sunday after Trinity.

Hymn 193.   II.   SALISBURY.

F ATHER of mercies, in Thy Word
　　What endless glory shines ;
For ever be Thy Name adored
　For these celestial lines.

Here springs of consolation rise,
　To cheer the fainting mind ;
And thirsty souls receive supplies,
　And sweet refreshment find.

O may these heavenly pages be
　Our ever new delight,
And still fresh beauties may we see,
　And still increasing light.

Divine Instructor, gracious Lord,
　Be Thou for ever near ;
Teach us to love Thy sacred Word,
　And find salvation there.

Twelfth Sunday after Trinity.

mn 194.   III.   ST. DAVID.

D moves in a mysterious way
His wonders to perform ;
ts His footsteps in the sea,
rides upon the storm.

unfathomable mines
ver-failing skill,
ures up His bright designs,
works His sovereign will.

ıl saints, fresh courage take :
louds ye so much dread
with mercy, and shall break
ssings on your head.

Judge not the Lord by feeble sense,
But trust Him for His grace :
Behind a frowning Providence
He hides a smiling face.

His purposes will ripen fast,
Unfolding every hour ;
The bud may have a bitter taste,
But sweet will be the flower.

Blind unbelief is sure to err,
And scan His work in vain ;
God is His own interpreter,
And He will make it plain.

Twelfth Sunday after Trinity.

COME, we that love the Lord,
 And let our joys be known,
Join in a song with sweet accord,
 And thus surround the throne.

The men of grace have found
 Glory begun below :
Celestial fruits on earthly ground
 From faith and hope may grow.

The hill of Zion yields
 A thousand sacred sweets,
Before we reach the heavenly fields,
 Or walk the golden streets.

Then let our songs abound,
 And every tear be dry ;
We're marching through Immanuel's ground
 To fairer worlds on high.

Thirteenth Sunday after Trinity.

Hymn 196.

DORT.

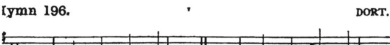

H OW beauteous are their feet
 Who stand on Zion's hill,
Who bring salvation on their tongues,
 And words of peace reveal.

How happy are our ears,
 That hear the joyful sound,
Which kings and prophets waited for,
 And sought, but never found.

How blessed are our eyes,
 That see this heavenly light ;
Prophets and kings desired it long,
 But died without the sight.

The Lord makes bare His arm
 Through all the earth abroad ;
Let every nation now behold
 Their Saviour and their God.

Thirteenth Sunday after Trinity.

Hymn 197.   II.   OLD 104TH.

O WORSHIP the King,
　　All glorious above ;
O gratefully sing
　　His power and His love ;
Our Shield and Defender,
　　The Ancient of days,
Pavilioned in splendour,
　　And girded with praise.

O tell of His might,
　　O sing of His grace,
Whose robe is the light,
　　Whose canopy space :
His chariots of wrath
　　Deep thunder-clouds form,
And dark is His path
　　On the wings of the storm.

Frail children of dust,
　　And feeble as frail,
In Thee do we trust,
　　Nor find Thee to fail :
Thy mercies how tender !
　　How firm to the end !
Our Maker, Defender,
　　Redeemer, and Friend !

O measureless Might !
　　Ineffable Love !
While angels delight
　　To hymn Thee above,
The humbler creation,
　　Though feeble their lays,
With true adoration
　　Shall lisp to Thy praise.

Thirteenth Sunday after Trinity.

Hymn 198.   III.   CONSTANCE.

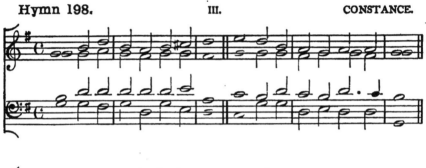

J ESUS, my All, to heaven is gone ;
    He that I placed my hopes upon ;
His track I see, and I'll pursue
The narrow way, till Him I view.

The way the holy Prophets went,
The way that leads from banishment,
The King's highway of holiness,
I'll go ; for all the paths are peace.

This is the way I long have sought,
And mourned because I found it not ;
My grief, my burden, long have been
Because I could not cease from sin.

Lo! glad I come; and Thou, dear Lamb,
Shall take me to Thee, as I am :
Nothing but sin I Thee can give ;
Yet help me, and Thy praise I'll live !

Thirteenth Sunday after Trinity.

Hymn 199.　　　　　IV.　　　　　CARISBROOK.

L O, round the throne, at God's right hand,
　The saints in countless myriads stand :
Of every tongue, redeemed to God,
Arrayed in garments washed in blood.

Through tribulation great they came;
They bore the cross, despised the shame :
From all their labours now they rest,
In God's eternal glory blest.

Hunger and thirst they feel no more ;
Nor sin, nor pain, nor death deplore ;
The tears are wiped from every eye,
And sorrow yields to endless joy.

They see their Saviour face to face,
And sing the triumphs of His grace;
Him day and night they ceaseless praise ;
To Him their loud hosannas raise.

Fourteenth Sunday after Trinity.

L ORD, whose love, in power excelling,
    Washed the leper's stain away,
Jesus, from Thy heavenly dwelling,
    Hear us, help us, when we pray.

From the filth of vice and folly,
    From infuriate passion's rage,
Evil thoughts and hopes unholy,
    Heedless youth and selfish age :

From the lusts whose deep pollutions
    Adam's ancient taint disclose,
From the Tempter's dark intrusions,
    Restless doubt and blind repose :

From the miser's cursed treasure,
    From the drunkard's jest obscene,
From the world, its pomp and pleasure,
    Jesus, Master, make us clean !

Fourteenth Sunday after Trinity.

ymn 201.   II.   EATON.

THOU Saviour, who Thyself didst give
That all the world might turn and live,
Who dost the careless sinner draw
With cords of love to Thy pure law,
Who dost Thy Church with fondness call,
And by Thy grace receivest all:

Behold us, Lord! before Thy throne,
Inspire and make our hearts Thine own:
Bind to Thy cross our wandering will,
Each act with holy purpose fill:
Our weakness let Thy strength defend,
Thou Author of our Faith, and End.

Fourteenth Sunday after Trinity.

Hymn 202.   III.   GLOUCESTER.

TRY us, O God, and search the
    ground
  Of every evil heart;
Whate'er of sin in us is found,
  O bid it all depart.

When to the right or left we stray,
  Pity Thy helpless sheep;
Bring back our feet into the way,
  And there Thy wanderers keep.

Help us to help each other, Lord,
  Each other's burden bear;
Let each his friendly aid afford,
  To sooth his brother's care.

Help us to build each other up,
  Help us ourselves to prove;
Increase our faith, confirm our hope,
  And perfect us in love.

Complete at length Thy work of grace,
  And take us to Thy rest,
Among Thy saints who see Thy face,
  To be for ever blest.

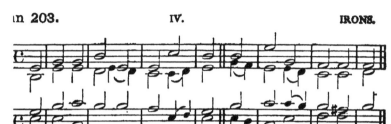

E, let us join our friends above
'hat have obtained the prize,
he eagle wings of love
s celestial rise.

e saints terrestrial sing,
hose to glory gone,
e servants of our King,
ı and heaven, are one.

y, we dwell in Him,
ıurch, above, beneath,
ow divided by the stream,
rrow stream of death.

One army of the living God,
  To His command we bow ;
Part of His host hath crossed the flood,
  And part is crossing now.

Our spirits too shall quickly join,
  Like them with glory crowned,
And shout to see our Captain's sign,
  To hear His trumpet sound.

O that we now might grasp our guide !
  O that the word were given !
Come, Lord of Hosts, the waves divide,
  And land us all in heaven\

Hymn 204.   I.   ST. PETER'S.

C OMMIT thou all thy griefs
    And ways into His hands,
To His sure truth and tender care
    Who earth and heaven commands :

Who points the clouds their course,
Whom winds and seas obey ;
He shall direct thy wandering feet,
He shall prepare thy way.

Thou on the Lord rely,
    So safe thou shalt go on :
Fix on His word thy stedfast eye,
    So shall thy work be done.

No profit canst thou gain
By self-consuming care :
To Him commend thy cause : His ear
Attends the softest prayer.

Thy everlasting truth,
Father, Thy ceaseless love,
Sees all Thy children's wants, and knows
What best for each will prove.

Fifteenth Sunday after Trinity.

Hymn 205.   II.   NEWPORT.

WHY should I fear the darkest
    hour,
Or tremble at the Tempter's power?
Jesus vouchsafes to be my Tower.

Though hot the fight, why quit the field?
Why must I either fly or yield,
Since Jesus is my mighty Shield?

When creature-comforts fade and die,
Worldlings may weep, but why should I?
Jesus still lives, and still is nigh.

Though all the flocks and herds were dead,
My soul a famine need no: dread,
For Jesus is my living Bread.

I know not what may soon betide,
Or how my wants shall be supplied;
But Jesus knows, and will provide.

Though sin would fill me with distress,
The throne of grace I dare address,
For Jesus is my Righteousness.

Though faint my prayers, and cold
    my love,
My stedfast hope shall not remove,
While Jesus intercedes above.

Against me earth and hell combine;
But on my side is Power divine;
Jesus is all, and He is mine.

Fifteenth Sunday after Trinity.

Hymn 206.   III.   HERRNHUTT.

O LORD, how happy should we be
　If we could cast our care on Thee,
If we from self could rest;
And feel at heart that One above
In perfect wisdom, perfect love,
　Is working for the best.

How far from this our daily life :—
How oft disturbed by anxious strife,
　By sudden wild alarms :
O could we but relinquish all
Our earthly props, and simply fall
　On Thine Almighty arms !

Could we but kneel and cast our load,
E'en while we pray, upon our God,
　Then rise with lightened cheer :
Sure that the Father who is nigh
To still the famished ravens' cry,
　Will hear in that we fear.

Fifteenth Sunday after Trinity.

IKE Noah's weary dove,
   That soared the earth around,
t a resting-place above
   cheerless waters found:

ase, my wandering soul,
   estless wing to roam:
wide world to either pole
not for thee a home.

Behold the ark of God,
   Behold the open door:
Hasten to gain that dear abode,
   And rove, my soul, no more.

There safe shalt thou abide,
   There sweet shall be thy rest,
And every longing satisfied,
   With full salvation blest.

And, when the waves of ire
   Again the earth shall fill,
The Ark shall ride the sea of fire:
   Then rest on Sion's hill.

Hymn 208.   L   KENBURY.

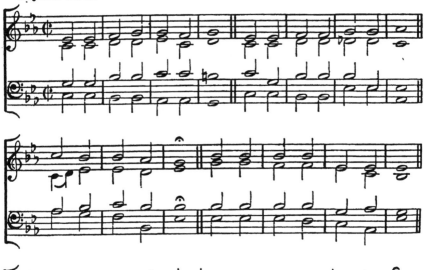

J ESUS, when I fainting lie,
   And the world is flitting by,
  Hold Thou up mine head :
When the cry is, "Thou must die,"
And the dread hour draweth nigh,
  Stand by my bed !

Jesus, when the worst is o'er,
  And they bear me from the door,
   Meet the sorrowing throng :
"Weep not !" let the mourner hear:
Widow's woe and orphan's tear
   Turn into song.

   Jesus ! in the last great day,
  Come Thou down and touch my clay,
    Speak the word, "Arise !"
  Friend to gladsome friend restore
  Living, praising evermore,
    Above the skies !

Sixteenth Sunday after Trinity.

Hymn 209.   II.   BADEN (SECOND FORM).

WHATE'ER my God ordains is
    right,
  Holy His will abideth ;
I will be still whate'er He doth,
  And follow where He guideth.
    He is my God,
    Though dark my road ;
He holds me that I shall not fall,
Wherefore to Him I leave it all.

Whate'er my God ordains is right,
  He never will deceive me :
He leads me by the proper path,
  I know He will not leave me,
    And take content
    What He hath sent :
His hand can turn my grief away,
And patiently I wait His day.

Whate'er my God ordains is right,
  Though now this cup in drinking
May bitter seem to my faint heart,
  I take it all unshrinking :
    Tears pass away
    With dawn of day :
Sweet comfort yet shall fill my heart,
And pain and sorrow shall depart.

Whate'er my God ordains is right,
  Here shall my stand be taken :
Though sorrow, need, or death be mine,
  Yet am I not forsaken :
    My Father's care
    Is round me there :
He holds me that I shall not fall,
And so to Him I leave it all.

Sixteenth Sunday after Trinity.

Hymn 210.   III.   LABRADOR.

O LET him whose sorrow
    No relief can find,
Trust in God, and borrow
    Ease for heart and mind.
Where the mourner, weeping,
    Sheds the secret tear,
God His watch is keeping,
    Though none else is near.

God will never leave us,
    All our wants He knows,
Feels the pains that grieve us,
    Sees our cares and woes :
When in grief we languish,
    He will dry the tear,
Who His children's anguish
    Soothes with succour near.

All our woe and sadness
    In this world below,
Balance not the gladness
    We in heaven shall know,
When our gracious Saviour
    In the realms above,
Crowns us with His favour,
    Fills us with His love.

Sixteenth Sunday after Trinity.

Hymn 211.   IV.   MAGDEBURG.

WHEN gathering clouds around I view,
And days are dark and friends are few,
On Him I lean, who not in vain
Experienced every human pain :
He sees my wants, allays my fears,
And counts and treasures up my tears.

If aught should tempt my soul to stray
From heavenly wisdom's narrow way :
To fly the good I would pursue,
Or do the sin I would not do:
Still He, who felt temptation's power,
Shall guard me in that dangerous hour.

If vexing thoughts within me rise,
And, sore dismayed, my spirit dies :
Still He, who once vouchsafed to bear
The sickening anguish of despair,
Shall sweetly soothe, shall gently dry,
The throbbing heart, the streaming eye.

And O, when I have safely past
Through every conflict but the last,
Still, still unchanging, watch beside
My painful bed, for Thou hast died :
Then point to realms of cloudless day,
And wipe the latest tear away.

n 212.   L.   ST. ANN'S.

S, exalted far on high, .
 whom a name is given,
surpassing every name
 known in earth or heaven ;

hose throne shall every knee
lown with one accord ;
hose throne shall every tongue
s that Thou art Lord ;

Jesus, who, in the form of God,
   Didst equal honour claim ;
Yet, to redeem our guilty souls,
   Didst stoop to death and shame.

O may that mind in us be formed,
   Which shone so bright in Thee ;
An humble, meek, and lowly mind,
   From pride and envy free.

    May we to others stoop, and learn
      To emulate Thy love ;
    So shall we bear Thine image here,
      And share Thy throne above.

Hymn 213.   II.   EZEKIEL.

O WHY on death so bent?
    Hast thou not heard a voice that cries,
"I joy not in the death of Him' that dies?"
    Then turn thee and repent.

Or is the heart yet hard,
And all too deep the guil'ty stain?
And seems it that the golden gates' remain
    To thee for ever barred?

That voice still sounds within;
The Spirit and the Bride' say, "Come:"
"Return, poor outcast, to thy Fa'ther's home,
    And leave the husks of sin."

Or wouldst thou yet awhile
Linger amidst thine emp'ty dreams,
Loving to sojourn where forbid'den streams
    Make fertile Sodom's soil?

Speeds on thy brief reprieve:
Not long shall sound the voice' that cries,
"I joy not in the death of him' that dies:"
    Then turn thyself, and live.

Seventeenth Sunday after Trinity.

Hymn 214.   III.   RATISBON.

HOLY Jesus, in whose Name
 Thou hast bid Thy servants claim
Of the Father's love, to grant
All the good they wish or want ;
Trusting in Thy Name alone,
Draw we near Thy Father's throne.

Holy Jesus, at whose Name,
Through this universal frame,
By the Almighty Sire's decree,
All its dwellers bow the knee ;
To Thy Father's Name we join
In co-equal worship Thine.

Son of Man, to whom is given,
With the majesty of heaven,
Partner Thou of man's estate,
For mankind to mediate :
Hear us, when to Thee we plead
For Thy flock to intercede.

Son of God, to whom of right,
Partner of Thy Father's might,
Sole, adorable, and true,
Empire o'er the world is due :
Hear us, when on Thee we call
For Thy blessing, Lord of all.

Seventeenth Sunday after Trinity.

Hymn 215.   IV.   MAYENNE.

Major, verses 1, 3, 4.

Minor, verse 2.

SON of Man, to Thee we cry :

 By the wondrous mystery

Of Thy dwelling here on earth,

By Thy pure and holy birth,—

Lord, Thy presence let us see,

Thou our Light and Saviour be.

Lamb of God, to Thee we cry :

By Thy bitter agony,

By Thy pangs to us unknown,

By Thy spirit's parting groan,

Lord, Thy presence let us see,

Thou our Light and Saviour be.

Prince of Life, to Thee we cry :

By Thy glorious majesty,

By Thy triumph o'er the grave,

By Thy power to help and save,

Lord, Thy presence let us see,

Thou our Light and Saviour be.

Lord of glory, God most high,

Man exalted to the sky,

With Thy love our bosom fill :

Help us to perform Thy will :

Then Thy glory we shall see,

Thou wilt bring us home to Thee.

Eighteenth Sunday after Trinity.

Hymn 216.

O BREAD to pilgrims given,
　　O food that angels eat,
O manna sent from heaven,
　　For heaven-born natures meet :
Give us, for Thee long-pining,
　　To eat till richly filled :
Till earth's delights resigning,
　　Our every wish is stilled.

O Water, life-bestowing,
　　From out the Saviour's heart,
A fountain purely flowing,
　　A fount of love Thou art,
O let us, freely tasting,
　　Our burning thirst assuage :
Thy sweetness, never wasting,
　　Avails from age to age.

Jesus, this Feast receiving,
　　We Thee unseen adore :
Thy faithful word believing,
　　We take, and doubt no more :
Give us, Thou True and Loving,
　　On earth to live by Thee :
Then, Death the veil removing,
　　Thy glorious Face to see.

Eighteenth Sunday after Trinity.

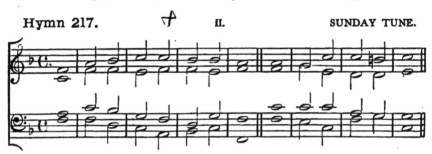

O THAT the Lord would guide my ways,
　To keep His statutes still ;
O that my God would grant me grace
　To know and do His will.

O send Thy Spirit down to write
　Thy law upon my heart :
Nor let my tongue indulge deceit,
　Nor act the liar's part.

From vanity turn off my eyes ;
　Let no corrupt design,
Nor covetous desires arise
　Within this soul of mine.

Order my footsteps by Thy word
　And make my heart sincere ;
Let sin have no dominion, Lord,
　But keep my conscience clear.

Make me to walk in Thy commands,
　'Tis a delightful road :
Nor let my head, or heart, or hands,
　Offend against my God.

Eighteenth Sunday after Trinity.

Hymn 218.   III.   HEREFORD.

O LORD, I would delight in Thee,
    And on Thy care depend :
To Thee in every trouble flee,
    My best, my only friend.

When all created streams are dried,
    Thy fulness is the same :
May I with this be satisfied,
    And glory in Thy Name.

No good in creatures can be found,
    But may be found in Thee :
I must have all things and abound,
    While God is good to me.

O that I had a stronger faith,
    To look within the veil ;
To credit what my Saviour saith,
    Whose word can never fail.

O Lord, I cast my care on Thee :
    I triumph and adore ;
Henceforth my great concern shall be
    To love and please Thee more.

Eighteenth Sunday after Trinity.

VOUCHSAFE Thy gracious pre-
     sence, Lord,
Dispose us now to hear Thy Word;
In meekness grant us to receive,
And with the heart its truths believe :
Thus, Lord, Thy waiting servants bless,
And crown Thy Gospel with success.

To us that sacred Word apply,
With sovereign power and energy ;
And cause us in Thy faith and fear
To practise all that we shall hear :
Thus, Lord, Thy waiting servants bless,
And crown Thy Gospel with success.

Father, in us Thy Son reveal,
Teach us to know and do Thy will :
Thy saving strength and love display,
And guide us to the realms of day :
Thus, Lord, Thy waiting servants bless,
And crown Thy Gospel with success.

Nineteenth Sunday after Trinity.

LORD, may we never, save to One,
   In worship bow the knee;
And never may we, Lord, forego
   The worship due to Thee.

Though Mammon should our hearts allure,
   Or Glory with her guiles,
Or Pleasure should our homage claim
   With fascinating smiles;

Though Satan, with his gilded pomps,
   Be by the world adored,
And flaming furnaces await
   The servants of the Lord;

Yet may we never, save to One,
   In worship bow the knee;
And never may we, Lord, forego
   The worship due to Thee.

Nineteenth Sunday after Trinity.

Hymn 221.   II.   TURNAU.

R OUND the Lord in glory seated,
   Cherubim and Seraphim
Filled His temple, and repeated
   Each to each the alternate hymn:

" Lord, Thy glory fills the heaven,
   Earth is with its fulness stored :
Unto Thee be glory given,
   Holy, Holy, Holy, Lord !"

Heaven is still with glory ringing,
   Earth takes up the angels' cry,
" Holy, Holy, Holy," singing,
   " Lord of Hosts, the Lord Most High!"

With His seraph train before Him,
   With His holy Church below,
Thus conspire we to adore Him,
   Bid we thus our anthem flow :

" Lord, Thy glory fills the heaven,
   Earth is with its fulness stored :
Unto Thee be glory given,
   Holy, Holy, Holy, Lord !"

Nineteenth Sunday after Trinity.

Hymn 222. III. BEDFORD.

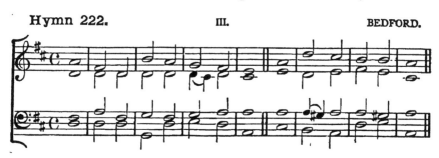

THROUGH all the changing scenes
 In trouble and in joy, [of life,
The praises of my God shall still
 My heart and tongue employ.

O magnify the Lord with me,
 With me exalt His Name :
When in distress to Him I called,
 He to my rescue came.

The hosts of God encamp around
 The dwellings of the just :
Deliverance He affords to all
 Who on His succour trust.

O make but trial of His love ;
 Experience will decide,
How blest are they, and only they,
 Who in His truth confide.

Fear Him, ye saints, and ye will then
 Have nothing else to fear :
Make you His service your delight,
 Your wants shall be His care.

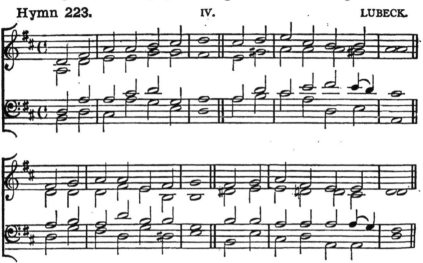

H EAVEN and earth, and sea and air,
   God's eternal praise declare :
Up, my soul, awake and raise
Grateful hymns and songs of praise.

See the sun, with glorious ray,
Pierce the clouds at opening day :
Moon and stars, in splendour bright,
Praise their God through silent night.

See how earth, with beauty decked,
Tells a heavenly Architect :
Spreading wood and budding flower,
Speak His wonder-working power.

See the billows tumbling o'er,
Chafing with incessant roar :
Hear them, as they sink or swell,
Loud their Maker's praises tell.

Through the world, great God, I trace
Wonders of Thy power and grace :
Write more deeply on my heart
What I am, and what Thou art.

Twentieth Sunday after Trinity.

PETERBOROUGH.

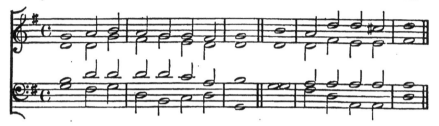

THOU, who hast called us by Thy word
    The marriage feast to share
Of Thy dear Son, our only Lord,
    Thy bidden guests prepare.

No vain excuse we dare to make,
    Thy call we do not slight ;
We come unworthy ; for His sake
    Help us to come aright.

The marriage garment we require
    Thyself to us impart,
And with Thy precious gifts inspire
    A pure and thankful heart.

Lord of the feast, our coming bless,
    And round our souls entwine
The garment of Thy righteousness,
    In which Thy saints shall shine.

Twentieth Sunday after Trinity.

Hymn 225.   II.   ELVEY.

THOU who art enthroned above,
Thou in whom we live and move,
Good it is with joyful tongue
To resound Thy praise in song :
When the morning paints the skies,
When the sparkling stars arise,
All Thy favours to rehearse,
And give thanks in grateful verse.

Sweet the day of sacred rest,
When devotion fires the breast,
When we dwell within Thy house,
Hear Thy Gospel, pay our vows,
Songs to heaven's high mansion raise,
Fill Thy courts with songs of praise,
And in psalms and hymns proclaim
Honours to Thy glorious Name.

From Thy works our joys arise,
O Thou only good and wise ;
Who Thy wonders can express ?
All Thy thoughts are fathomless :
Warm our hearts with sacred fire,
And with songs of praise inspire ;
All our powers with all their might
Ever in Thy praise unite.

Twentieth Sunday after Trinity.

CHILDREN of the heavenly King,
As ye journey sweetly sing ;
Sing your Saviour's worthy praise,
Glorious in His works and ways.

We are travelling home to God,
In the way the fathers trod :
They are happy now, and we
Soon their happiness shall see.

Shout, ye little flock and blest,
You on Jesus' throne shall rest ;
There your seat is now prepared,
There your kingdom and reward.

Fear not, brethren, joyful stand
On the borders of your land ;
Jesus Christ, your Father's Son,
Bids you undismayed go on.

Lord, obediently we go,
Gladly leaving all below ;
Only Thou our leader be,
And we still will follow Thee.

Hymn 227.　　　　　　　IV.　　　　　　BOCHASTLE.

YE servants of the Lord,
　　Each in his office wait,
Observant of His heavenly word,
　　And watchful at His gate.

Let all your lamps be bright,
　　And trim the golden flame:
Gird up your loins as in His sight,
　　For awful is His Name.

Watch, 'tis the Lord's command;
　　And while we speak, He's near:
Mark the first signal of His hand,
　　And ready all appear.

O happy servant he
　　In such a posture found
He shall His Lord with rapture see,
　　And be with honour crowned.

Christ shall the banquet spread
　　With His own royal hand;
And raise that faithful servant's head
　　Amidst the angelic band.

Twenty-First Sunday after Trinity.

Hymn 228.

EIN' FESTE BURG.

A TOWER of strength is God our Lord,
A sure defence and trusty guard
His help as yet in every need
From danger hath our spirit freed:
  Our ancient foe in rage
    May all his spite display:
  May war against us wage,
    And arm him for the fray,
    He that can keep all earth at bay.

Weak is our unassisted power,
Defeated soon in peril's hour:
But on our side, and for the right,
The man of God's own choice doth fight;
  Jesus, the Christ, whose Name
    Exalted is on high,
  The Lord of Hosts, the same
    That reigneth in the sky,
    He giveth us the victory.

Twenty-First Sunday after Trinity.

Hymn 229.   II.   EASTHAM.

TEN thousand times ten thousand,
　　In sparkling raiment bright,
The armies of the ransomed saints
　　Throng up the steeps of light :
'Tis finished—all is finished,
　　Their fight with death and sin :
Fling open wide the golden gates,
　　And let the victors in !

What rush of Hallelujahs
　　Fills all the earth and sky !
What ringing of a thousand harps
　　Bespeaks the triumph nigh !
O day, for which Creation
　　And all its tribes were made :
O joy, for all its former woes
　　A thousand fold repaid !

O then what raptured greetings
　　On Canaan's happy shore,
What knitting severed friendships up,
　　Where partings are no more !
Then eyes with joy shall sparkle,
　　That brimmed with tears of late :
Orphans no longer fatherless,
　　Nor widows desolate.

Twenty-First Sunday after Trinity.

Hymn 230.   III.   ST. MICHAEL.

SOLDIERS of Christ, arise,
　　And put your armour on;
Strong in the strength which God supplies
　Through His eternal Son.

Stand boldly in His might,
　With all His strength endued;
And take, to arm you for the fight,
　The armour of your God.

From strength to strength go on,
　Wrestle, and fight, and pray;
Tread all the powers of darkness down,
　And win the well-fought day.

That, having all things done,
　And all your conflicts past,
You may o'ercome through Christ alone,
　And stand entire at last.

Twenty-First Sunday after Trinity.

ETERNAL source of every joy,
  Well may Thy praise our lips employ,
ile in Thy temple we appear,
ose goodness crowns the circling year.

flowery spring at Thy command
balms the air and paints the land ;
summer rays with vigour shine,
raise the corn, and cheer the vine.

Thy hand in autumn richly pours
Through all our coasts redundant stores,
And winters, softened by Thy care,
No more a face of horror wear.

Seasons and months and weeks and days
Demand successive songs of praise ;
Still be the cheerful homage paid
With opening light and evening shade.

O may our more harmonious tongues
In worlds unknown pursue the songs :
And in those brighter courts adore,
Where days and years revolve no more.

Twenty-Second Sunday after Trinity.

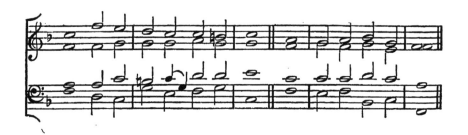

LORD, as to Thy dear Cross we flee,
  And plead to be forgiven,
So let Thy life our pattern be,
  And form our souls for heaven.

Help us through good report and ill,
  Our daily cross to bear,
Like Thee to do our Father's will,
  Our brethren's griefs to share.

Let grace our selfishness expel,
  Our earthliness refine,
And kindness in our bosoms dwell,
  As free and true as Thine.

If joy shall at Thy bidding fly,
  And grief's dark day come on,
We in our turn would meekly cry,
  " Father, Thy will be done."

Kept peaceful in the midst of strife,
  Forgiving and forgiven,
O may we lead the pilgrim's life,
  And follow Thee to heaven.

Twenty-Second Sunday after Trinity.

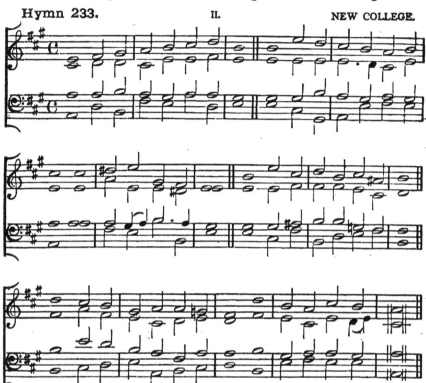

THERE is a dwelling-place above ;
  Thither to meet the God of love,
   The poor in spirit go :
There is a paradise of rest ;
For contrite hearts and souls distrest
   Its streams of comfort flow.

There is a voice to mercy true;
To them who mercy's path pursue
   That voice shall bliss impart:
There is a sight from man concealed ;
That sight, the face of God revealed,
   Shall bless the pure in heart.

There is a name in heaven bestowed
That name, which hails them sons of God,
   The friends of peace shall know :
There is a kingdom in the sky,
Where they shall reign with God on high,
   Who serve Him here below.

Hymn 234.　　　　　　　III.　　　　　　　EATINGTON.

LORD, it belongs not to my care
　　Whether I die or live :
To love and serve Thee is my share,
　　And this Thy grace must give.

If life be long, my days are blest,
　　When they are spent for Thee :
If short my course, I sooner rest,
　　From sin and trouble free.

Come, Lord, when grace hath made me
　　Thy blessed face to see :　　[meet
For if Thy work on earth be sweet,
　　What will Thy glory be ?

Then I shall end my sad complaints
　　And weary sinful days,
And join with the triumphant saints
　　Who sing Jehovah's praise.

My knowledge of that life is small :
　　The eye of faith is dim :
But 'tis enough that Christ knows all,
　　And I shall be with Him.

Twenty-Second Sunday after Trinity.

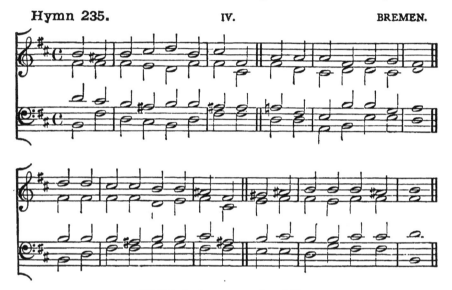

SEE the leaves around us falling,
  Dry and withered to the ground,
Thus to thoughtless mortals calling,
  In a sad and solemn sound :

Sons of Adam, once in Eden,
  Blighted when like us he fell,
Hear the lecture we are reading,
  'Tis, alas, the truth we tell.

Yearly in our course returning,
  Messengers of shortest stay,
Thus we preach this truth concerning,
  "Heaven and earth shall pass away."

On the Tree of life eternal,
  Man, let all thy hopes be laid,
Which alone, for ever vernal,
  Bears a leaf that shall not fade.

Twenty-Third Sunday after Trinity.

Hymn 236.

GOLDBACH.

THOU hast a temple founded,
　Thy Church, on Thee the Rock :
By Faith securely grounded,
　She stands the tempest's shock :
Her stones are all united
　By the cement of Love :
Her spire of Hope is lighted
　By sunbeams from above.

The Cross is on her portal,
　Which, with Thy blood baptized,
Invites to joys immortal
　The world evangelized :
Thy grace is ever flowing
　Throughout that temple bright,
A temple ever growing
　In heavenly life and light.

Lord, make us by Thy merit,
　There lively stones to be :
Compacted by Thy Spirit
　In bonds of unity :
Jewels to deck for ever
　The mural diadem
Which crowns the crystal river
　Of new Jerusalem.

Twenty-Third Sunday after Trinity.

Hymn 237.   II.   KNARESBOROUGH.

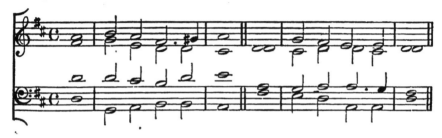

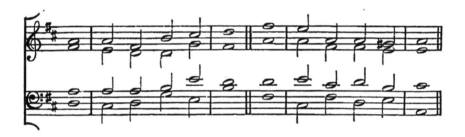

JERUSALEM on high
The saints' own city is,
Their home whene'er they die,
The centre of their bliss:
O happy place!
When shall I be,
My God, with Thee,
And see Thy face?

The patriarchs of old
  There from their travels cease :
The prophets there behold
  Their longed-for Prince of Peace :
    O happy place !
      When shall I be,
      My God, with Thee,
    And see Thy face ?

The Lamb's apostles there
  I might with joy behold :
And harpers I might hear
  Harping on harps of gold.
    O happy place !
      When shall I be,
      My God, with Thee,
    And see Thy face ?

There, too, the martyr band
  Who life in death have found,
Near to the King they stand,
  Their scars with glory crowned :
    O happy place !
      When shall I be,
      My God, with Thee,
    And see Thy face ?

There dwells my Lord and King,
  Judged here unfit to live :
There angels to Him sing,
  And cheerful homage give :
    O happy place !
      When shall I be,
      My God, with Thee,
    And see Thy face ?

Hymn 238.　　　　　III.　　　　　TALLIS'S CANON.

WHAT sinners value, I resign :
　Lord, 'tis enough that Thou art mine :
I shall behold Thy blissful Face,
And stand complete in righteousness.

O glorious hour, O blest abode !
I shall be near and like my God :
And flesh and sin no more control
The sacred pleasures of my soul.

My flesh shall slumber in the ground,
Till the last trumpet's joyful sound :
Then burst the chains with sweet surprise.
And in my Saviour's image rise.

Twenty-Third Sunday after Trinity.

F AIR vision! how thy distant gleam
    Brighten's Time's saddest hue :
Far fairer than the fairest dream,
    And yet how strangely true!

With thee in view, how poor appear
    The world's most winning smiles :
Vain is the tempter's subtlest snare,
    And vain hell's varied wiles.

Then welcome toil and care and pain,
    And welcome sorrow too :
All toil is rest, all grief is gain,
    With such a prize in view.

Come crown and throne, come robe and
    palm,
    Burst forth, glad stream of peace :
Come, holy city of the Lamb!
    Rise, Sun of Righteousness!

When shall the clouds that veil thy rays
    For ever be withdrawn ?
Why dost thou tarry, day of days?
    When shall thy gladness dawn?

Hymn 240.   COLMAR.

O PURIFY my soul from stain,
All tendencies to ill restrain ;
My soul with warm devotion fire,
Which may with sighs and groans aspire ;
Invigorate me when afraid,
When weak, vouchsafe me heavenly aid.

Truth sacred in my memory keep ;
For sin create contrition deep ;
All filial grace in me excite ;
Be witness that I walk aright ;
Seal pardon for transgressions past ;
Support me, when I breathe my last !

Twenty-fourth Sunday after Trinity.

SAINTS die, and we should gently weep;
   Sweetly in Jesus' arms they sleep;
Far from this world of sin and woe,
Nor sin, nor pain, nor grief, they know.

Death is a sleep; and O how sweet
To souls prepared its stroke to meet!
Their dying beds, their graves are blest,
For all to them is peace and rest.

Soon shall the earth's remotest bound
Feel the Archangel's trumpet sound;
Then shall the grave's dark caverns shake,
And joyful all the saints shall wake.

Bodies and souls shall then unite,
Arrayed in glory, strong and bright;
And all His saints will Jesus bring
His face to see, His love to sing.

Hymn 242. III. LUDLOW.

F OR all Thy saints, O Lord,
 Who strove in Thee to live,
Who followed Thee, obeyed, adored,
 Our grateful hymn receive.

For all Thy saints, O Lord,
 Accept our thankful cry,
Who counted Thee their great reward,
 And strove in Thee to die.

They all, in life and death,
 With Thee, their Lord, in view,
Learned from Thy Holy Spirit's breath
 To suffer and to do.

For this Thy Name we bless,
 And humbly beg that we
May follow them in holiness,
 And live and die in Thee.

Hymn 243.   IV.   TRANBY.

PRAISE the Lord; ye heavens adore Him,
    Praise Him angels in the height;
Sun and moon rejoice before Him,
    Praise Him all ye stars and light.

Praise the Lord, for He hath spoken,
    Worlds His mighty voice obeyed;
Laws which never shall be broken
    For their guidance He hath made.

Praise the Lord, for He is glorious,
    Never shall His promise fail;
He hath made His saints victorious,
    Sin and death shall not prevail.

Praise the God of our salvation,
    Evermore His power proclaim;
Heaven and earth and all creation
    Laud and magnify His Name.

Twenty-Fifth Sunday after Trinity.

Hymn 244. 　　　　L. 　　　　FRENCH.

WE all, O Lord, unrighteous are
　　With sorrow we confess
Our great and grievous sins to Thee,
　　The Lord our Righteousness.

Thou, Christ, the great Jehovah art,
　　The Fount of Holiness:
And, God with us, Thou art become
　　The Lord our Righteousness.

Washed are we with Thy precious Blood,
　　Clothed with Thy spotless dress:
O may we ever dwell in Thee
　　The Lord our Righteousness.

Make us to be in every deed
　　What we in word profess:
O make us like unto Thyself,
　　The Lord our Righteousness.

*N.B.—The Hymns for the Twenty-fifth Sunday after Trinity are to be used together with the Collect, Epistle,
and Gospel, on the Sunday next preceding Advent.*

Twenty-Fifth Sunday after Trinity.

BRETHREN, let us join to bless
Christ, the Lord our Righteousness:
Let our praise to Him be given,
High at God's right hand in heaven.

Son of God, to Thee we bow :
Thou art Lord and only Thou :
Thou the blessed Virgin's seed,
Glory of Thy Church, and Head.

Thee the angels ceaseless sing :
Thee we praise, our Priest and King :
Worthy is Thy Name of praise,
Full of glory, full of grace.

Thou hast the glad tidings brought
Of salvation by Thee wrought :
Wrought to set Thy people free ;
Wrought to bring our souls to Thee.

May we follow and adore
Thee, our Saviour, more and more :
Guide and bless us with Thy love,
Till we join Thy saints above.

Twenty-Fifth Sunday after Trinity.

Hymn 246.   III.   OLD 124TH.

OUR year of grace is wearing to its close,
  Its autumn storms are louring from the sky :
  Shine on us with Thy light, O God Most High :
Abide with us where'er our pathway goes,
Our guide in toil, our guardian in repose.

All through the months hath beamed Thy cheering light,
  From Bethlehem's Day-star waxing ever on :
  Through every cloud Thy blessed Sun hath shone :
Earth may be dark to them that walk by sight,
But for Thy Church the day is always bright.

Light us in life, that we may see Thy will,
  The track Thine Hand hath ordered for our way :
  Light us, when shadows gather o'er our day :
Shine on us in that passage lone and chill,—
And then our darkness with Thy glory fill.

Praise be to God from earth's remotest coast,
  From lands and seas, and each created race :
  Praise from the worlds His hand hath launched in space :
Praise from the Church, and from the heavenly host :
Praise to the Father, Son, and Holy Ghost.

Twenty-Fifth Sunday after Trinity.

Hymn 247.　　　✠　　　IV.　　　　　　KENT.

O GOD of Bethel, by whose hand
　　Thy people still are fed,
Who through this weary pilgrimage
　　Hast all our fathers led ;

Our vows, our prayers, we now present
　　Before Thy throne of grace ;
God of our fathers ! be the God
　　Of their succeeding race.

Through each perplexing path of life
　　Our wandering footsteps guide ;
Give us each day our daily bread,
　　And raiment fit provide.

O spread Thy covering wings around,
　　Till all our wanderings cease,
And at our Father's loved abode
　　Our souls arrive in peace !

Such blessings from Thy gracious hand
Our humble prayers implore ;
And Thou shalt be our chosen God,
And portion evermore.

St. Andrew's Day.

EISLEBEN.

OF all the honours man may wear,
  Of all his titles proudly stored,
No lowly palm this name shall bear,
  "The first to follow Christ the Lord."

Such name thou hast, who didst incline,
  Fired with the great Forerunner's joy,
Homeward to track the steps divine,
  And watch the Saviour's blest employ.

Lord, give to us Thy servants' grace
  To hear whene'er Thy preachers speak :
When Thou commandest, "Seek my Face,"
  Thy Face in earnest hope to seek.

Thus with the glorious company
  Of Thine Apostles may we raise
Through all eternity to Thee
  Glad hymns of never-ending praise.

St. Thomas the Apostle.

Hymn 249.

LONDON NEW.

W E walk by faith and not by sight ;
    No gracious words we hear
From Him who spoke as never man,
    But we believe Him near.

We may not touch His hands and side,
    Nor follow where He trod ;
But in His promise we rejoice,
    And cry " My Lord and God."

Help Thou, O Lord, our unbelief :
    And may our faith abound,
To call on Thee when Thou art near,
    And seek, where Thou art found :

That when our life of faith is done,
    In realms of clearer light
We may behold Thee as Thou art,
    With full and endless sight.

The Conversion of St. Paul.

NOTTINGHAM.

THE great Apostle, called by grace,
  Weaned from all works beside,
Preached the same faith he once abhorred,
  And Christ, whom he denied.

In perils and in troubles oft,
  His toilsome life he passed ;
But He who turned his heart at first,
  Upheld him to the last.

A chosen vessel of His will,
  He fought the fight of faith ;
And gained the crown of righteousness,
  Obedient unto death.

Thus, Lord of grace, to all Thy will
  Obedient may we be ;
And follow meekly in his steps,
  Even as he followed Thee.

The Purification of St. Mary.

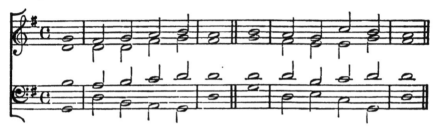

" BLEST are the pure in heart,
    For they shall see our God;
The secret of the Lord is theirs,
    Their soul is Christ's abode."

Might mortal thought presume
    To guess an angel's lay,
Such are the notes that echo through
    The courts of heaven to-day.

Such the triumphal hymns
    On Sion's Prince that wait,
In high procession passing on
    Towards His temple-gate.

Wide open from that hour
    The temple-gates are set,
And still the saints rejoicing there
    The holy Child have met.

Still to the lowly soul
    He doth Himself impart,
And for His cradle and His throne
    Chooseth the pure in heart.

St. Matthias's Day.

HOWARD.

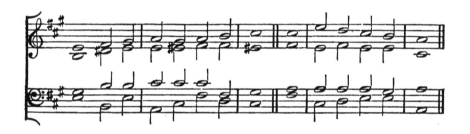

THE highest and the holiest place
    Guards not the heart from sin ;
The church that safest seems without
    May harbour foes within.

Thus in the small and chosen band
    Beloved above the rest,
One fell from his apostleship,
    A traitor-soul unblest.

But not the great designs of God
    Man's sin shall overthrow ;
Another witness to the truth
    Forth to the lands shall go.

Righteous, O Lord, are all Thy ways ;
    Long as the worlds endure,
From foes without and foes within
    Thy Church shall stand secure ;

The soul that sinneth, it shall die ;
But Thine shall never fail ;
The word of grace no less shall sound,
The truth no less prevail.

The Annunciation of the Blessed Virgin Mary.

Hymn 253.

POTSDAM.

THE first sad hours of shame
　One promise bright bestow ;
The woman's Seed shall rise at length,
　And bruise the deadly foe.

Where sin abounded once,
　Grace shall abound much more ;
Woman, that first gave ear to sin,
　The great Redeemer bore.

Blest was her favoured womb,
　Happy her sacred breast ;
The sojourn of the Lord of life,
　And where His lips were prest.

But doubly blest are they
　Who hear and keep His will ;
In them by faith is Jesus formed,
　And dwells within them still.

And still the gracious words
　To each believer sound :
" Hail, highly-favoured ; with the Lord
　Thou hast acceptance found."

St. Mark's Day.

HAYES'S 127TH.

CHRIST'S everlasting messengers,
  Who from the opening skies,
Traverse the earth in showers of light,
  And sow with mysteries!

The things discerned by seers of old,
  Behind the shadowy screen,
In the full day have ye beheld,
  With not a veil between.

The things which God as Man hath borne
  Which Man as God hath done,
Ye write as God dictates to all
  Who see the circling sun.

Though far in space and time apart,
  One Spirit sways you all;
And we in those blest characters
  Hear now that living call.

Glory to God, the Three in One,
  All glory be to Thee,
Who from our darkness callest us
  Thy glorious light to see.

St. Philip and St. James's Day.

Hymn 255.

O JESU Lord, the Way, the Truth,
    The Life, the Crown of all
Who here on earth confess Thy Name ;
    O hear us when we call !

We bring to mind with grateful joy
    Thy servants who of old
Withstood the snares of earth and hell,
    And now Thy face behold ;

Who sought on earth the joys of prayer,
    And that communion knew,
Which saints and angels share above
    With those who seek it too.

Vouchsafe us, Lord, we pray Thee now,
    To us it may be given,
Like them to live and die in Thee,
    And with Thee rise to heaven.

St. Barnabas the Apostle.

Hymn 256.

BRASTED.

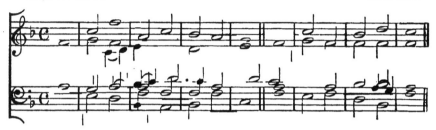

BRIGHTLY did the light divine
From his words and actions shine,
Whom the Twelve, with love unblamed,
" Son of Consolation " named.

Full of peace and lively joy,
Sped he on his high employ :
By his mild exhorting word
Adding many to the Lord.

Blessed Spirit, who didst call
Barnabas and holy Paul,
And didst them with gifts endue,
Mighty words and wisdom true :

Grant us, Lord of life, to be,
By their pattern, full of Thee :
That beside them we may stand,
In that day, on Christ's right hand.

St. John the Baptist's Day.

Hymn 257.

CAEN.

Second Tune.

ST. GABRIEL.

HERALD, in the wilderness
    Breaking up the road,
Sinking mountains, raising plains,
    For the path of God :

Prophet, to the multitudes
    Calling to repent ;
In the way of righteousness
    Unto Israel sent :

Messenger, God's chosen One
    Foremost to proclaim,
Proffered titles putting by,
    Pointing to the Lamb :

Captive, for the word of truth
    Boldly witnessing,
Then in Herod's dungeon-cave
    Faint and languishing :

Martyr, sacrificed to sin
    At that feast of shame,
As his life foreshewed the Lord,
    In his death the same,—

Holy Jesus, when He heard,
    Went apart to pray :
Thus may we our lesson take
    From His Saint to-day.

St. Peter's Day.

CRASSELIUS.

WHEN, within sight of danger's hour,
We boast of self-possessing power,
Teach us, O Lord, betimes to know
How weak are we, how strong the foe.

And when, beset by snares around,
Faithless to Thee our hearts are found,
Look Thou upon us, and renew
Our wandering thoughts, our vows untrue.

Then though Thou doubt us, and our love
By question and temptation prove ;
Faithful to Thee we shall abide,
In honour, as in weakness tried.

St. James the Apostle.

ST. MICHAEL.

O WHAT, if we are Christ's,
  Is earthly shame or loss?
Bright shall the crown of glory be,
  When we have borne the cross.

Keen was the trial once,
  Bitter the cup of woe,
Where martyred saints, baptized in blood,
  Christ's sufferings shared below.

Bright is their glory now,
  Boundless their joy above,
Where, on the bosom of their God,
  They rest in perfect love.

Lord! may that grace be ours,
  Like them in faith to bear
All that of sorrow, grief, or pain,
  May be our portion here.

Enough, if Thou at last
  The word of blessing give,
And let us rest beneath Thy feet
  Where saints and angels live.

St. Bartholomew the Apostle.

Hymn 260.

ST. MILDRED'S.

B LESSED are they whose hearts are
    pure,
  From guile their spirits free :
To them shall God reveal Himself,
  They shall His glory see.

Who in meek faith unmixed with doubt
  The engrafted word receive,
Whom the first sign of heavenly Power
  Persuades, and they believe :

Their simple souls upon His word
  In fullest light of love
Place all their trust, and ask no more
  Than guidance from above.

They, as they walk the painful world,
  See hidden glories rise :
Our God the sunshine of His love
  Unfolds before their eyes.

For them far greater things than these
  Doth Christ the Lord prepare :
Whose bliss no heart of man can reach,
  No human voice declare.

St. Matthew the Apostle.

NARENZA.

" Arise and follow Me ! "
Who answers to the call ?
Not Ruler, Scribe, or Pharisee,
Proud and regardless all.

" Arise and follow Me ! "
The Publican hath heard :
And by the deep Gennesaret sea
Obeys the Master's word.

Thenceforth in joy or fear,
Where'er the Saviour trod,
Among the Twelve his place was near
The Holy One of God.

His is no honour mean,
For Christ to write and die :
Apostle, Saint, Evangelist,
His record is on high.

St. Michael and all Angels.

MERTON COLLEGE.

THEY are evermore around us,
   Though unseen to mortal sight,
In the golden hour of sunshine,
   And in sorrow's starless night,
Deepening earth's most sacred pleasures
   With the peace of sin forgiven,
Whispering to the lonely mourner
   Of the painless joys of Heaven.

Lovingly they come to help us,
   When our faith is cold and weak,
Guiding us along the pathway
   To the blessed Home we seek :
In our hearts we hear their voices,
   Breathing sympathy and love,
Echoes of the spirit language
   In the sinless world above.

They are with us in the conflict,
   With their words of hope and cheer
When the Foe of our salvation
   And his armèd hosts draw near :
And a greater One is with us,
   And we shrink not from the strife,
While the Lord of angels leads us
   On the battle-field of life.

St. Luke the Evangelist.

Hymn 263.

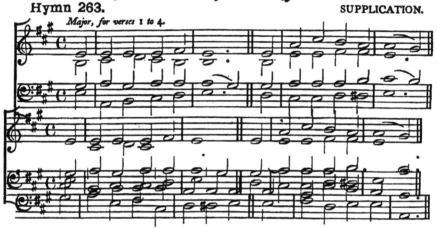

Major, for verses 1 to 4.

L IFT high the song of praise
   For him whose holy pen
Gave down the hymns of other days
   To glad the sons of men.

Glory to God on high,
   And peace upon the earth,
Goodwill to men be now proclaimed,
   As at the Saviour's birth.

The Lord to magnify,
   Be lifted every voice,
And in our God and Saviour
   Let every soul rejoice.

With benedictions high
   Let Israel's God be praised :
Who hath salvation's mighty horn
   Up for His people raised.

Minor, for verse 5.

And when around our path
The call of Death is heard,

Lord, let Thou us depart in peace,
   According to Thy word.

Simon and St. Jude, Apostles.

L ET the Church of God rejoice
    For the Apostles' fostering care,
For the sounding of their voice,
    For their preaching and their prayer :

Whom the Lord our God did choose
    To the farthest lands to go :
Whom the Husbandman did use
    Holiest seed on earth to sow.

In the new Jerusalem,
    Twelve foundations firm are laid ;
On the Apostles of the Lamb
    Is the glorious structure stayed.

Firmly built on them, may we,
    Bound to Christ, our Corner Stone,
In the heavenly temple be,
    One in heart, in doctrine one.

All Saints' Day.

Hymn 265.   SEIR.

WHAT are these in bright array,
    This innumerable throng,
Round the altar, night and day,
    Hymning one triumphant song?
"Worthy is the Lamb once slain,
    Blessing, honour, glory, power,
Wisdom, riches to obtain,
    New dominion every hour."

These through fiery trials trod;
    These from great affliction came;
Now, before the Throne of God,
    Sealed with His Almighty Name,
Clad in raiment pure and white,
    Victor-palms in every hand,
Through their dear Redeemer's might,
    More than conquerors they stand.

Hunger, thirst, disease unknown,
    On immortal fruit they feed;
Them the Lamb amidst the Throne
    Shall to living fountains lead:
Joy and gladness banish sighs;
    Perfect love dispels all fear;
And for ever from their eyes
    God shall wipe away the tear.

Missions.

CEYLON.

FROM Greenland's icy mountains,
  From India's coral strand,
Where Afric's sunny fountains
  Roll down their golden sand,
From many an ancient river,
  From many a palmy plain,
They call us to deliver
  Their land from error's chain.

What though the spicy breezes
  Blow soft o'er Ceylon's isle ;
Though every prospect pleases,
  And only man is vile ;
In vain with lavish kindness
  The gifts of God are strown,
The heathen in his blindness
  Bows down to wood and stone.

Can we, whose souls are lighted
  With wisdom from on high,
Can we to men benighted
  The lamp of life deny ?
Salvation ! O Salvation !
  The joyful sound proclaim,
Till each remotest nation
  Has learnt Messiah's Name.

Waft, waft, ye winds, His story,
  And you, ye waters, roll,
Till, like a sea of glory,
  It spreads from pole to pole ;
Till o'er our ransomed nature
  The Lamb for sinners slain,
Redeemer, King, Creator,
  In bliss returns to reign.

Missions.

Hymn 267.   II.   MECKLENBURGH.

WORD by God the Father sent,
Lord of All, Omnipotent:
Word for sinners' need supplied,
As their comfort and their guide:
Word of our Redeemer's grace,
Who, to save our sinful race,
Of our guilt to pay the price,
Gave Himself a Sacrifice:

Word of God the Spirit's might,
Who our heavenward course doth light,
Prompteth good, and by His breath
What He prompts accomplisheth:
Word of life, both pure and strong,
Word for which the heathen long:
Spread abroad, till out of night
All the world awake to light.

Up! for lo, earth's surface o'er
Waving fields with ripening store:
Countless sheaves are spread around,
Few, O few, the reapers found!
Lord of Harvest, great and kind,
Rouse to action heart and mind:
Let the gathering nations all
See Thy light and hear Thy call.

Missions.

FROM all that dwell below the skies
　　Let the Creator's praise arise :
Let the Redeemer's Name be sung
Through every land, by every tongue.

Eternal are Thy mercies, Lord :
Eternal truth attends Thy word :
Thy praise shall sound from shore to shore,
Till suns shall rise and set no more.

JESUS, immortal King, display
   Thine arm of strength, and win the day;
Let all Thy foes astonished flee,
And leave the conquered world to Thee.

Gird on Thy thigh Thy conquering sword,
Victorious King, most mighty Lord;
Finish the work Thou hast begun,
And let Thy will on earth be done.

Let heavenly hosts triumphant sing,
The Lord Omnipotent is King;
Let all His saints rejoice at this:
The kingdoms of the world are His.

Praise God, from whom all blessings flow;
Praise Him all creatures here below:
Praise Him above, ye heavenly host:
Praise Father, Son, and Holy Ghost.

Missions.

JESUS, Thy Church with longing eyes
    For Thy expected coming waits:
When will the promised light arise,
    And glory beam from Zion's gates?

Ev'n now, when tempests round us fall,
    And wintry clouds o'ercast the sky,
Thy words with pleasure we recall,
    And deem that our redemption's nigh.

Come, gracious Lord, our hearts renew,
    Our foes repel, our wrongs redress,
Man's rooted enmity subdue,
    And crown Thy Gospel with success.

O come, and reign o'er every land:
    Let Satan from his throne be hurled:
All nations bow to Thy command,
    And grace revive a dying world.

Missions (to the Jews).

O THAT the Lord's salvation
　　Were out of Zion come,
To heal His ancient nation,
　　To lead His outcasts home !

How long the holy city
　　Shall heathen feet profane ?
Return, O Lord, in pity,
　　Rebuild her walls again.

Let fall Thy rod of terror :
　　Thy saving grace impart :
Roll back the veil of error :
　　Release the fettered heart.

Let Israel, home returning,
　　Her lost Messiah see :
Give oil of joy for mourning,
　　And bind Thy Church to Thee.

Ordination.

TALLIS'S VENI CREATOR.

After the 4th verse.

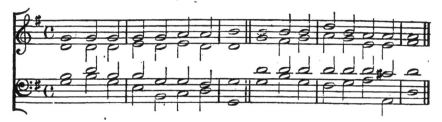

After the 4th verse.

COME, Holy Ghost, our souls inspire,
  And lighten with celestial fire.
Thou the anointing Spirit art,
Who dost Thy sevenfold gifts impart.

Thy blessed unction from above
Is comfort, life, and fire of love.
Enable with perpetual light
The dulness of our blinded sight.

Anoint and cheer our soiled face
With the abundance of Thy grace ;
Keep far our foes, give peace at home,
Where Thou art guide no ill can come.

Teach us to know the Father, Son,
And Thee, of both, to be but One,
That, through the ages all along,
This may be our endless song :
    Praise to Thy eternal merit,
    Father, Son, and Holy Spirit.

* This tune is especially intended for Antiphonal use : see Rubric in the Ordering of Priests.

Ordination.

POUR out Thy Spirit from on high,
  Lord, Thine ordained servants bless :
Graces and gifts to each supply,   [ness.
  And clothe Thy priests with righteous-

Within Thy temple as they stand,
  To teach the truth as taught by Thee,
Saviour, like stars in Thy right hand,
  Let all Thy Church's pastors be.

Wisdom and zeal and love impart,
  Firmness with meekness from above,
To bear Thy people in their heart,
  And love the souls whom Thou
    dost love :

To love and pray and never faint,
  By day and night strict guard to keep,
To warn the sinner, cheer the saint,
  Nourish Thy lambs, and feed Thy sheep.

Then, when their work is finished here,
  May they in hope their charge resign :
When the chief Shepherd shall appear,
  May they, O God, in glory shine.

Ordination.

ME, Holy Ghost, eternal God,
Proceeding from above,
om the Father and the Son,
God of peace and love ;

r minds, into our hearts
heavenly grace inspire ;
ith and godliness we may
ie with full desire.

t the very Comforter
ief and all distress ;
ivenly gift of God most high,
ingue can it express ;

The fountain and the living spring
Of joy celestial ;
The fire so bright, the love so sweet,
The unction spiritual.

Thou in Thy gifts art manifold,
By them Christ's church doth stand :
In faithful hearts Thou writ'st Thy law,
The finger of God's hand.

According to Thy promise, Lord,
Thou givest speech with grace ;
That thro' Thy help God's praises may
Resound in every place.

O Holy Ghost, into our minds
Send down Thy heavenly light ;
Kindle our hearts with fervent zeal,
To serve God day and night.

Harvest.

ELVEY.

COME, ye thankful people, come,
    Raise the song of Harvest-home !
All is safely gathered in,
Ere the winter storms begin :
God our Maker doth provide
For our wants to be supplied :—
Come to God's own temple, come,
Raise the song of Harvest-home !

All the world is God's own field,
Fruit unto His praise to yield ;
Wheat and tares together sown,
Unto joy or sorrow grown :
First the blade, and then the ear,
Then the full corn shall appear :
Lord of Harvest, grant that we
Wholesome grain and pure may be.

For the Lord our God shall come,
And shall take His Harvest home :
From His field shall in that day
All offences purge away :
Give His angels charge at last
In the fire the tares to cast ;
But the fruitful ears to store
In His garner evermore.

Even so, Lord, quickly come,
To Thy final Harvest-home ;
Gather Thou Thy people in,
Free from sorrow, free from sin ;
There for ever purified,
In Thy presence to abide :
Come, with all Thine angels, come,
Raise the glorious Harvest-home !

Harvest.

PRAISE to God, immortal praise,
  For the love that crowns our days :
Bounteous Source of every joy,
Let Thy praise our tongues employ.
For the blessings of the field,
For the stores the gardens yield :
Flocks that whiten all the plain :
Yellow sheaves of ripened grain :

All that Spring with bounteous hand
Scatters o'er the smiling land :
All that liberal Autumn pours
From her rich o'er-flowing stores :
These to Thee, our God, we owe,
Source whence all our blessings flow :
And for these our soul shall raise
Grateful vows and solemn praise.

Yet, should rising whirlwinds tear
From its stem the ripening ear :
Should the fig-tree's blasted shoot
Drop her green untimely fruit :
Should the vine put forth no more,
Nor the olive yield her store :
Though the sickening flocks should fall,
And the herds desert the stall :

Should Thine altered hand restrain
The early and the latter rain,
Blast each opening bud of joy,
And the rising year destroy :
Yet to Thee our soul should raise
Grateful vows and solemn praise :
And, when every blessing's flown,
Love Thee for Thyself alone.

Harvest.

G REAT God, to Thee our songs we raise,
    To Thee devote our grateful praise :
O never may our footsteps rove
From Thee, the source of truth and love :
But may we still Thy praise proclaim,
And joy in our Redeemer's Name.

What though the fig-tree shall decay,
Fruitless the vine shall waste away,
Although the olive shall not bear,
Nor corn produce the ripened ear,
Yet still may we Thy praise proclaim,
And joy in our Redeemer's Name.

Though in our folds no flocks be found,
Nor bud to deck the exhausted ground,
Though all the hopes of plenty fail,
Though blighting pestilence prevail,
Yet may we still Thy praise proclaim,
And joy in our Redeemer's Name.

Harvest.

OUR hearts and voices let us raise,
In songs of thankfulness and praise,
Our heavenly Father's love to bless,
Which crowns the year with fruitfulness.

For what Thy bounteous hand imparts,
Give us the grace of thankful hearts,
Hearts which their thankfulness may prove
By hymns of praise and gifts of love.

Cheered by Thy sun and fostering rain,
The valleys wave with golden grain,
The corn-fields teem with ripened shocks,
The stalls with herds, the folds with flocks.

O Thou that art the Harvest's Lord,
Send forth the sowers of Thy Word :
And may we speed them on the wings
Of prayer and cheerful offerings.

May distant climes Thy Word receive,
Land after land, till all believe,
And bear the fruit that never dies :
Till earth shall bloom like Paradise.

Day of Thanksgiving.

L IFT up to God the voice of praise,
　Whose breath our souls inspired :
Loud and more loud the anthem raise,
　With grateful ardour fired.

Lift up to God the voice of praise,
　Whose tender care sustains
Our feeble frame, encompassed round
　With death's unnumbered pains.

Lift up to God the voice of praise,
　Whose goodness, passing thought,
Loads every minute as it flies
　With benefits unsought.

Lift up to God the voice of praise,
　From whom salvation flows :
Who sent His Son our souls to save
　From everlasting woes.

Lift up to God the voice of praise,
　For hope's transporting ray,
That lights through darkest shades of death
　To realms of endless day.

Day of Thanksgiving.

NOW thank we all our God,
With heart, and hands, and voices;
Who wondrous things hath done,
In whom His world rejoices :
Who from our mother's arms
Hath blessed us on our way
With countless gifts of love,
And still is ours to-day.

O may this bounteous God
Through all our life be near us ;
With ever joyful hearts
And blessed peace to cheer us :
And help us in His grace,
And guide us when perplext :
And free us from all ills
In this world and the next.

All praise and thanks to God
The Father now be given,
The Son, and Him who reigns
With Them in highest heaven :
The one eternal God
Whom heaven and earth adore ;
For thus it was, is now,
And shall be evermore.

Day of Thanksgiving.

PRAISE the Lord, His glories shew,
Saints within His courts below,
Angels round His throne above,
All that see and share His love.

Earth to heaven and heaven to earth
Tell His wonders, sing His worth:
Age to age, and shore to shore,
Praise Him, praise Him, evermore!

Praise the Lord, His mercies trace:
Praise His providence and grace;
All that He for man hath done,
All He sends us through His Son:

Strings and voices, hands and hearts,
In the concert bear your parts:
All that breathe, your Lord adore,
Praise Him, praise Him, evermore.

Day of Thanksgiving.

T HOU God, all glory, honour, power,
　　Art worthy to receive :
Since all things by Thy power were made,
　And by Thy bounty live.

And worthy is the Lamb all power,
　Honour and wealth to gain,
Glory and strength : who for our sins
　A sacrifice was slain.

All worthy Thou who hast redeemed
　And ransomed us to God,
From every nation, every coast,
　By Thy most precious blood.

Blessing and honour, glory, power,
　By all in earth and heaven,
To Him that sits upon the throne,
　And to the Lamb be given.

Hymn 283.

ST. MATTHEW.

G REAT King of nations, hear our prayer, while at Thy feet we fall,
And humbly with united cry to Thee for mercy call :
The guilt is ours, but grace is Thine, O turn us not away,
But hear us from Thy lofty throne, and help us when we pray.

Our fathers' sins were manifold, and ours no less we own,
Yet wondrously from age to age Thy goodness hath been shown,
When dangers, like a stormy sea, beset our country round,
To Thee we looked, to Thee we cried, and help in Thee was found.

With one consent we meekly bow beneath Thy chastening hand,
And pouring forth confession meet, mourn with our mourning land :
With pitying eye behold our need, as thus we lift our prayer,
Correct us with Thy judgments, Lord, then let Thy mercy spare.

Day of Humiliation.

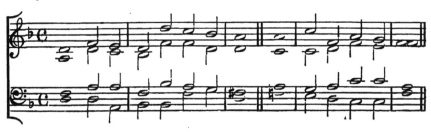

ALMIGHTY Lord, before Thy throne
   Thy mourning people bend,
For on Thy pardoning grace alone
   Our prostrate hopes depend.

Dire judgments from Thy heavy hand
   Thy dreadful power display;
Yet mercy spares our guilty land,
   And still we live to pray.

O turn us, turn us, mighty Lord,
   By Thy subduing grace;
So shall our hearts obey Thy Word,
   And we shall see Thy face.

If famine, plague, or foes invade,
   We shall not sink or fear,
Secure of all-sufficient aid
   When God, our God, is near.

Day of Humiliation.

O UT of the deep we call to Thee :
   Lord we are weak and faint :
O let Thine ears consider well
   The voice of our complaint.

Wert Thou our sins extreme to mark,
   O Lord, who should be spared ?
But there is mercy with Thee, Lord,
   Therefore Thou shalt be feared.

We look for Thee ; our spirits wait :
   Our trust is in Thy Word :
Even before the morning watch
   We flee unto the Lord.

Day of Humiliation.

Hymn 286.

BEDFORD (Minor).

O LORD, when storms around us howl,
 And all is dark and drear,
In all the tempests of the soul,
 O blessed Jesu, hear!

In hours of sin and deep distress,
 O shew us, Lord, Thy face:
In penitential loneliness,
 O give us, Jesu, grace!

In days when faith will scarce be found,
 And wolves be in the fold,
When sin and sorrow will abound,
 And charity wax cold:

Then hear Thy saints who to Thee pray
 To bring them to their home:
Hear, when Thy waiting people say,
 "Come, blessed Jesu, come!"

The Queen's Accession.

SAVOY.

O KING of Kings, Thy blessing shed
On our anointed Sovereign's head ;
And, looking from Thy throne in heaven,
Protect the crown Thyself hast given.

Her, for Thy sake, may we obey ;
Uphold her right, and love her sway ;
Rememb'ring that the powers that be
Are ministers ordained by Thee.

By her this favoured nation bless ;
To all her counsels give success ;
In peace, in war, Thine aid be seen ;
Confirm her strength : O save our Queen!

And O, when earthly thrones decay,
And earthly kingdoms fade away,
Give her a nobler throne on high,
A crown of immortality.

Holy Baptism.

Hymn 288.   TALLIS'S ORDINAL.

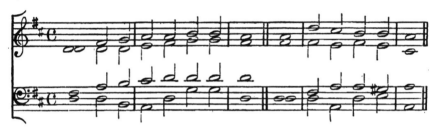

I N token that thou shalt not fear
　　Christ crucified to own,
We print the Cross upon thee here,
　　And stamp thee His alone.

In token that thou shalt not blush
　　To glory in His Name,
We blazon here upon thy front
　　His glory and His shame.

In token that thou shalt not flinch
　　Christ's quarrel to maintain,
But 'neath His banner manfully
　　Firm at thy post remain ;

In token that thou too shalt tread
　　The path He travelled by,
Endure the Cross, despise the shame,
　　And sit thee down on high ;

Thus outwardly and visibly
　　We seal thee for His own ;
And may the brow that wears His Cross
　　Hereafter share His crown.

Holy Baptism.

OUR children, Lord, in faith and prayer
   We now present to Thee;
Let them Thy covenant mercies share,
   And Thy salvation see.

Such helpless babes Thou didst embrace,
   While dwelling here below,
To us and ours, O God of grace,
   The same compassion shew.

In early days their hearts secure
   From worldly snares, we pray,
And may they to the end endure
   In every righteous way.

Before them let their parents live
   In Godly faith and fear,
Then first to heaven their souls receive,
   Next bring their children there.

Confirmation.

Hymn 290.

SEPHAR.

GOD of mercy, throned on high,
  Listen from Thy lofty seat ;
Hear, O hear our feeble cry,
  Guide, O guide our wandering feet.

Young and erring travellers, we
  All our dangers do not know ;
Scarcely fear the stormy sea,
  Hardly feel the tempest blow.

Jesus, lover of the young,
  Cleanse us with Thy Blood divine :
Ere the tide of sin grow strong,
  Save us, keep us, make us Thine.

When perplexed in danger's snare,
  Thou alone our guide canst be ;
When oppressed with woe and care,
  Whom have we to trust but Thee ?

Let us ever hear Thy voice,
  Ask Thy counsel every day ;
Saints and angels will rejoice,
  If we walk in wisdom's way.

Saviour, give us faith, and pour
  Hope and love on every soul :
Hope, till time shall be no more ;
  Love, while endless ages roll.

Confirmation.

FAIR waved the golden corn
   In Canaan's pleasant land,
When full of joy some shining morn
   Went forth the reaper-band.

To God, so good and great,
   Their cheerful thanks they pour,
Then carry to His temple gate
   The choicest of their store.

For thus the holy word,
   Spoken by Moses, ran—
" The first ripe ears are for the Lord,
   The rest He gives to man."

Like Israel, Lord, we give
   Our earliest fruits to Thee,
And pray that, long as we shall live,
   We may Thy children be.

Thine is our youthful prime,
   And life and all its powers :
Be with us in our morning time,
   And bless our evening hours.

In wisdom let us grow
   As years and strength are given,
That we may serve Thy Church below,
   And join Thy saints in heaven.

Holy Communion.

I. ROCKINGHAM.

MY God, and is Thy table spread?
　　And does Thy cup with love o'erflow?
Thither be all Thy children led,
　　And let them all its sweetness know.

Hail, sacred feast, which Jesus makes,
　　Rich banquet of His flesh and blood!
Thrice happy he, who here partakes
　　That sacred stream, that heavenly food.

Why are its dainties all in vain
　　Before unwilling hearts displayed?
Was not for you the Victim slain?
　　Are you forbid the children's bread?

O let Thy table honoured be,
　　And furnished well with joyful guests:
And may each soul salvation see,
　　That here its sacred pledges tastes.

Holy Communion.

BREAD of heaven, on Thee we feed,
  For Thy flesh is meat indeed ;
Ever may our souls be fed
With this true and living bread :
Day by day with strength supplied
Through the life of Him who died.

Vine of heaven, Thy Blood supplies
This blest cup of sacrifice :
Lord, Thy wounds our healing give ;
To Thy Cross we look and live :
Jesu, may we ever be
Grafted, rooted, built in Thee.

Holy Matrimony.

Hymn 294.   EASTHAM.

THE voice that breathed o'er Eden,
　　That earliest wedding day,
The primal marriage blessing,
　　It hath not passed away :
Still in the pure espousal
　　Of Christian man and maid,
The Holy Three are with us,
　　The threefold grace is said :

For dower of blessed children,
　　For love and faith's sweet sake,
For high mysterious union
　　Which nought on earth may break :
Be present, awful Father,
　　To give away this bride,
As Eve Thou gav'st to Adam,
　　Out of His own pierced side :

Be present, Son of Mary,
　　To join their loving hands,
As Thou didst join two natures
　　In Thine eternal bands :
Be present, Holiest Spirit,
　　To bless them as they kneel,
As Thou for Christ, the Bridegroom,
　　The heavenly Spouse dost seal.

Holy Matrimony.

Hymn 295.   II.   MERTON COLLEGE.

LORD and Father of creation,
  From Thy heavenly throne above,
Make Thy face to shine upon them,
  Deign to bless their plighted love :
Through the world to bless and keep them,
  Though the evil way be wide,
Give them strength, as on they journey,
  With Thy light their footsteps guide.

To the bride, beyond her beauty,
  Give her still Thy grace to know :
To the bridegroom, for her portion,
  On her heavenly gifts bestow.
So their bridal gifts shall never
  Fade, as earthly things decay,
But the bride and bridegroom ever
  Walk together in Thy way.

Burial of the Dead.

I.

ALTORF.

ETERNITY! eternity!
How long art thou, eternity!
A moment's pleasure sinners know,
Through which they pass to endless woe:
A moment's woe the righteous taste,
Through which to endless joys they haste:
  Mark well, O man, eternity.

Eternity! eternity!
  Awful art thou, eternity!
Who looks to thee, alone is wise:
Sin's pleasures all he can despise.
The world attracts him now no more,
His love for vain delights is o'er:
  His thoughts are on eternity.

Eternity! eternity!
How dreadful is eternity!
O Thou eternal King and God,
Here, prove us with Thy chastening rod;
Here, let us all Thy judgments bear;
Hereafter, Lord, in mercy spare:
  Oh, spare us in eternity.

Burial of the Dead.

AT length released from many woes,
How sweetly dost thou sleep;
How calm and peaceful Thy repose,
While Christ thy soul doth keep.

In earth's wide field thy body now
We sow, which lifeless lies,
In sure and certain hope that thou
More glorious shalt arise.

Then rest thee in thy lowly bed,
Nor shall our hearts repine :
Thy toils and woes are finished ;
A happy lot is thine.

The Bridegroom will not long delay,
The Shepherd soon will come,
And take His cherished lamb away
To His eternal home.

Burial of the Dead.

LIE down, frail body, here,
　　Earth has no fairer bed,
No gentler pillow to afford :
　Come, rest thy home-sick head.

A sky without a cloud,
A sea without a wave,
These are but shadows of thy rest
　In this thy peaceful grave.

Rest for the toiling hand,
Rest for the thought-worn brow,
Rest for the weary way-sore feet,
　Rest from all labour now.

Rest for the fevered brain,
Rest for the throbbing eye :　　[more
Through these parched lips of thine no
　Shall pass the moan or sigh.

Soon shall the trump of God
Give out the welcome sound,
That shakes thy silent chamber walls,
　And breaks the turf-sealed ground.

'Twas sown in weakness here ;
'Twill then be raised in power :
That which was sown an earthly seed,
　Shall rise a heavenly flower.

Consecration of a Church.

Hymn 299.   STUTTGART.

LORD, whose temple once did glisten
  With a monarch's rich supplies,
To our humbler praises listen,
  Bless our willing sacrifice :
Be our votive offering given
  To the Father and the Son,
Sweeter in the sight of heaven
  Than the scents of Lebanon.

Clouds and darkness veiled Thy dwelling
  In Thine earthly house of old,
Though the hymn of praise was swelling
  'Mid the pomp of Ophir's gold :
Here Thy love our hearts shall brighten,
  Hence ye earth-born clouds away !
Here Thy Spirit shall enlighten,
  Shining to the perfect day.

Hither on the Sabbath-morning,
  Guide us on our Church-way-path ;
Here, O Lord, in life's first dawning,
  Sprinkle every child of wrath ;
Here around Thine altar bending,
  Feed us with the living bread :
Here, to wait their Lord's descending
  Hallowed earth, receive the dead.

When our Israel's sore transgression
  Stops the windows of the sky,
When we sink beneath oppression,
  When we see our thousands die ;
Father, when we here adore Thee
  In Thy house, our prayer receive :
When we spread our hands before Thee
  Here behold us, and forgive.

Consecration of a Church.

CHRIST is our Corner-stone,
  On Him alone we build :
With His true saints alone
  The courts of Heaven are filled :
    On His great love
      Our hopes we place
      Of present grace,
    And joys above.

O then with hymns of praise
  These hallowed courts shall ring :
Our voices we will raise
  The Three in One to sing
    And thus proclaim
      In joyful song,
      Both loud and long,
    That glorious Name.

Here, gracious God, do Thou
  For evermore draw nigh,
Accept each faithful vow,
  And mark each suppliant sigh :
    In copious shower
      On all who pray
      Each holy day
    Thy blessing pour.

Here may we gain from heaven
  The grace which we implore,
And may that grace, once given,
  Be with us evermore :
    Until that day
      When all the blest
      To endless rest
    Are called away.

Consecration of a Church.

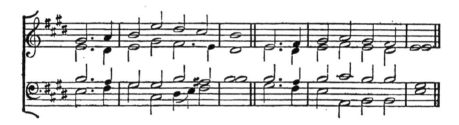

LORD of Hosts! to Thee we raise
    Here a house of prayer and praise :
Thou Thy people's hearts prepare
Here to meet for praise and prayer.

Let the living here be fed
With Thy Word, the heavenly bread ;
Here, in hope of glory best,
May the dead be laid to rest.

Here to Thee a temple stand
While the sea shall gird the land :
Here reveal Thy mercy sure
While the sun and moon endure.

Hallelujah ! earth and sky
To the joyful sound reply :
Hallelujah ! hence ascend
Prayer and praise till time shall end.

Consecration of a Church.

THIS stone to Thee in faith we lay ;
 We build the temple, Lord, to Thee ;
Thine eye be open night and day,
 To guard this house and sanctuary.

Here, when Thy people seek Thy face,
 And dying sinners pray to live,
Hear Thou in heaven, Thy dwelling-place,
 'And, when Thou hearest, O forgive.

Here, when Thy messengers proclaim
 The blessed Gospel of Thy Son,
Still, by the power of His great Name,
 Be mighty signs and wonders done.

But will, indeed, Jehovah deign
 Here to abide, no transient guest ?
Here will the world's Redeemer reign ?
 And here the Holy Spirit rest ?

That glory never hence depart,
 Yet choose not, Lord, this house alone ;
Thy kingdom come to every heart,
 In every bosom fix Thy throne.

For a School Anniversary.

Hymn 303. BADEN.

WHEN in the Lord Jehovah's name,
The Saviour lowly riding came,
Loudest and first an infant throng
Greeted His coming with their song,
   Hosanna in the highest.

We too are taught to know the Lord,
To fear His name, to read His word,
And though we simple are and young,
Can praise Him with our joyful song,
   Hosanna in the highest.

Soon shall the Lord again pass by,
To judgment from His throne on high;
And from the saints' assembled throng,
Shall burst upon the world the song,
   Hosanna in the highest.

Then may our youthful band be found
With coronals of triumph crowned;
Raising, the heavenly hosts among,
Our chorus of eternal song,
   Hosanna in the highest.

B B 2

Almsgiving.

FATHER of mercies, send Thy grace
   All-powerful from above,
To form in our obedient souls
   The image of Thy love.

O may our sympathizing breast
   That generous pleasure know,
Freely to share in others' joy,
   And weep for others' woe.

Whene'er the helpless sons of grief
   In low distress are laid,
Soft be our hearts their pains to feel,
   And swift our hands to aid.

So Jesus looked on dying man,
   Enthroned above the skies;
And when He saw their lost estate,
   Felt His compassion rise.

Since Christ, to save our guilty souls,
   On wings of mercy flew,
We, whom the Saviour thus hath loved,
   Should love each other too.

Almsgiving.

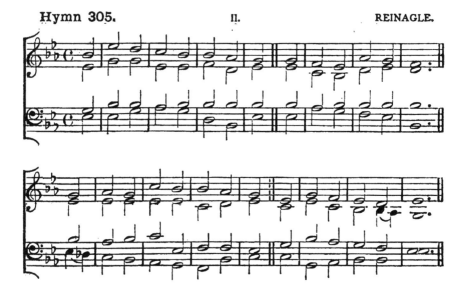

FOUNTAIN of good! to own Thy love
   Our thankful hearts incline ;
What can we render, Lord, to Thee,
   When all the worlds are Thine ?

But Thou hast needy brethren here,
   Partakers of Thy grace,
Whose humble names Thou wilt confess
   Before Thy Father's face.

In their sad accents of distress
   Thy pleading voice is heard,
In them Thou mayest be clothed and fed,
   And visited and cheered.

Thy face, with reverence and with love,
   We in Thy poor would see,
For while we minister to them,
   We do it, Lord, to Thee.

Morning.

EPPENDORF.

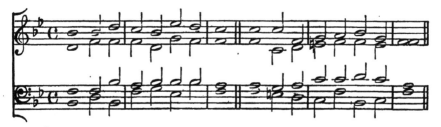

A WAKE, my soul, and with the sun
    Thy daily stage of duty run :
Shake off dull sloth, and early rise
To pay thy morning sacrifice.

Thy previous time mis-spent redeem :
Each present day thy last esteem :
Improve thy talent with due care :
For the great day thyself prepare.

In conversation be sincere,
  Keep conscience as the noontide clear :
Think how All-seeing God thy ways
And all thy secret thoughts surveys.

Lord, I my vows to Thee renew,
Disperse my sins as morning dew :
Guard my first springs of thought and will,
And with Thyself my spirit fill.

Direct, control, suggest this day
All I design, or do, or say :
That all my powers, with all their might,
In Thy sole glory may unite.

Praise God from whom all blessings flow,
Praise Him all creatures here below :
Praise Him above, ye heavenly host,
Praise Father, Son, and Holy Ghost.

Morning.

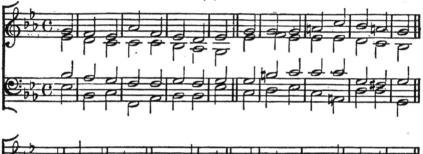

N OW hath arisen the star of day,
　　And with his rising let us pray
That we throughout his course be freed
From sinful thought and hurtful deed.

O may the Lord our tongues restrain
From sounding strife and converse vain ;
And from His servants' eyesight hide
The toys of vanity and pride.

May He our inner thoughts make pure,
From sins presumptuous us secure,
Grant us to use such abstinence
As may subdue the things of sense.

That we, when night succeeds to day,
And this bright sun hath past away,
Unspotted from the world may raise
To God our Saviour songs of praise.

Morning.

O JESU, Lord of heavenly grace,
    Thou brightness of Thy Father's
Thou fountain of eternal light,   [face,
Whose beams disperse the shades of night :

Come, holy Sun of heavenly love,
Shower down Thy radiance from above :
And to our inward hearts convey
The Holy Spirit's cloudless ray.

May faith, deep-rooted in the soul,
Subdue our flesh, our minds control :
May guile depart, and discord cease,
And all within be joy and peace.

O hallowed be the approaching day !
Let meekness be our morning ray,
And faithful love our noonday light,
And hope our sunset, calm and bright.

O Christ, with each returning morn,
Thine image to our hearts is borne :
O may we ever clearly see
Our Saviour and our God in Thee.

Morning.

M Y God, how endless is Thy love,
    Thy gifts are every evening new,
And morning mercies from above
    Gently distil like early dew.

Thou spread'st the curtains of the night,
    Great Guardian of my sleeping hours :
Thy sovereign word restores the light,
    And quickens all my drowsy powers.

I yield my powers to Thy command,
    To Thee I consecrate my days :
Perpetual blessings from Thy hand
    Demand perpetual songs of praise.

Morning.

CHRIST, whose glory fills the skies,
  Christ, the true, the only Light,
Sun of Righteousness, arise,
  Triumph o'er the shades of night:
Day-spring from on high, be near,
Day-star, in my heart appear.

Dark and cheerless is the morn
  Unaccompanied by Thee;
Joyless is the day's return,
  Till Thy mercy's beams I see;
Till they inward light impart,
Glad my eyes, and warm my heart.

Visit, then, this soul of mine,
  Pierce the gloom of sin and grief:
Fill me, Radiancy Divine,
  Scatter all my unbelief:
More and more Thyself display,
Shining to the perfect day.

Morning.

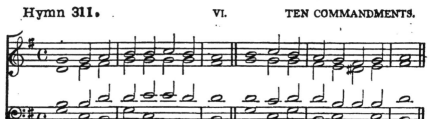

FORTH in Thy Name, O Lord, I go,
  My daily labour to pursue,
Thee, only Thee, resolved to know,
  In all I think, or speak, or do.

The task Thy wisdom hath assigned
  O let me cheerfully fulfil;
In all my works Thy presence find,
  And prove Thine acceptable will.

Preserve me from my calling's snare,
  And hide my simple heart above,
Above the thorns of choking care,
  The gilded baits of worldly love.

Thee may I set at my right hand,
  Whose eyes mine inmost substance see,
And labour on at Thy command,
  And offer all my works to Thee.

Give me to bear Thy easy yoke,
  And every moment watch and pray;
And still to things eternal look,
  And hasten to Thy glorious day;

For Thee delightfully employ   [given,
  Whate'er Thy bounteous grace hath
And run my course with even joy,
  And closely walk with Thee to heaven.

Evening.

TALLIS'S CANON.

ALL praise to Thee, my God, this night,
For all the blessings of the light :
Keep me, O keep me, King of kings,
Beneath Thine own Almighty wings !

Forgive me, Lord, for Thy dear Son,
The ill that I this day have done :
That with the world, myself, and Thee,
I, ere I sleep, at peace may be.

Teach me to live that I may dread
The grave as little as my bed :
To die that this vile body may
Rise glorious at the awful day.

O may my soul on Thee repose,
And may sweet sleep mine eyelids close :
Sleep that may me more vigorous make
To serve my God when I awake.

When in the night I sleepless lie,
My soul with heavenly thoughts supply :
Let no ill dreams disturb my rest,
No powers of darkness me molest.

Praise God from whom all blessings flow,
Praise Him, all creatures here below :
Praise Him above, ye heavenly host :
Praise Father, Son, and Holy Ghost.

Evening.

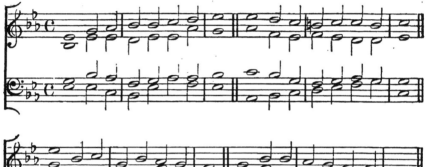

SUNK is the sun's last beam of light,
  And darkness wraps the world in night:
Christ, light us with Thy heavenly ray,
Nor let our feet in darkness stray.

Thanks, Lord, that Thou throughout the day
Hast kept all grief and harm away :
That angels tarried round about
Our coming in and going out.

Whate'er of wrong we've done or said,
Let not on us the charge be laid ;
That through Thy free forgiveness blest,
In peaceful slumber we may rest.

Thy guardian angels round us place,
All evil from our couch to chase :
Both soul and body, while we sleep,
In safety, gracious Father, keep.

Evening.

S UN of my soul, Thou Saviour dear,
   It is not night if Thou be near :
O may no earth-born cloud arise
To hide Thee from Thy servant's eyes.

When the soft dews of kindly sleep
My weary eyelids gently steep,
Be my last thought, how sweet to rest
For ever on my Saviour's breast.

Abide with me from morn till eve,
For without Thee I cannot live :
Abide with me when night is nigh,
For without Thee I dare not die.

Evening.

THROUGH the day Thy love has spared us,
　Wearied, we lie down to rest:
Through the silent watches guard us,
　Let no foe our peace molest:
　　　Jesus, Thou our Guardian be:
　　　Sweet it is to trust in Thee.

Pilgrims here on earth and strangers,
　Dwelling in the midst of foes,
Us and ours preserve from dangers,
　In Thy love may we repose:
　　　And when life's sad day is past,
　　　Rest with Thee in heaven at last.

Evening.

V. UPSAL.

GOD, that madest earth and heaven,
    Darkness and light,
Who the day for toil hast given,
    For rest the night,
May Thine angel-guards defend us,
Slumber sweet Thy mercy send us,
Holy dreams and hopes attend us,
    This live-long night.

Evening.

SWEET Saviour, bless us ere we go:
　　Thy word into our minds instil,
And make our lukewarm hearts to glow
　　With lowly love and fervent will.
　　　　Through life's long day and death's
　　　　　　dark night,
　　　O gentle Jesus, be our Light.

The day is done, its hours have run,
　　And Thou hast taken count of all,
The scanty triumphs grace hath won,
　　The broken vow, the frequent fall.
　　　　Through life's long day and death's
　　　　　　dark night,
　　　O gentle Jesus, be our Light.

Sweet Saviour, bless us: night is come:
　　Through night and darkness near us be:
Good angels watch about our home,
　　And we are one day nearer Thee.
　　　　Through life's long day and death's dark night,
　　　O gentle Jesus, be our Light.

Evening.

ABIDE with me: fast falls the eventide:
The darkness deepens: Lord, with me abide:
When other helpers fail, and comforts flee,
Help of the helpless, O abide with me.

Swift to its close ebbs out life's little day:
Earth's joys grow dim, its glories pass away:
Change and decay in all around I see:
O Thou who changest not, abide with me.

I need Thy presence every passing hour:
What but Thy grace can foil the tempter's power?
Who like Thyself my guide and stay can be?
Through cloud and sunshine, O abide with me.

I fear no foe with Thee at hand to bless:
Ills have no weight, and tears no bitterness:
Where is death's sting? where, grave, thy victory?
I triumph still, if Thou abide with me.

Hold Thou Thy Cross before my closing eyes:
Shine through the gloom, and point me to the skies:
Heaven's morning breaks, and earth's vain shadows flee;
In life and death, O Lord, abide with me.

Parting.

DOWLAND.

PART in peace! Christ's life was peace,
 Let us live our life in Him:
Part in peace! Christ's death was peace,
 Let us die our death in Him.

Part in peace! Christ promise gave
Of a life beyond the grave,
Where all mortal partings cease:
Brethren, sisters, part in peace.

Family Meeting.

SAVIOUR of them that trust in Thee,
 Once more, with supplicating cries,
We lift the heart, and bend the knee,
 And bid devotion's incense rise.

For mercies past we praise Thee, Lord,—
 The fruits of earth, the hopes of heaven;
Thy helping arm, Thy guiding Word,
 And answered prayers, and sins forgiven.

Whene'er we tread on danger's height,
 Or walk temptation's slippery way,
Be still, to steer our steps aright, [stay.
 Thy Word our guide, Thine arm our

Be ours Thy fear and favour still,
 United hearts, unchanging love;
No scheme that contradicts Thy will,
 No wish that centres not above.

And since we must be parted here,
 Support us when the hour shall come:
Wipe gently off the mourner's tear,
 Rejoin us in our heavenly home.

In time of War.

CANNONS.

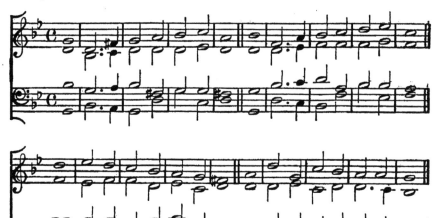

O GOD of love, O King of peace !
    Make wars throughout the world to cease :
The wrath of sinful men restrain ;
Give peace, O God, give peace again !

Remember, Lord, Thy works of old,
The wonders that our fathers told ;
Remember not our sins' dark stain :
Give peace, O God, give peace again !

Whom shall we trust but Thee, O Lord ?
Where rest but on Thy faithful word ?
None ever called on Thee in vain ;
Give peace, O God, give peace again !

Where saints and angels dwell above,
All hearts are knit in holy love ;
O bind us in that heavenly chain ;
Give peace, O God, give peace again !

Psalm C.

ALL people that on earth do dwell,
  Sing to the Lord with cheerful voice,
Him serve with fear, His praise forth tell :
  Come ye before Him and rejoice.

The Lord, ye know, is God indeed,
  Without our aid He did us make :
We are His flock, He doth us feed ;
  And for His sheep He doth us take.

O enter then His gates with praise,
  Approach with joy His courts unto :
Praise, laud and bless His name always,
  For it is seemly so to do.

For why ? the Lord our God is good,
  His mercy is for ever sure :
His truth at all times firmly stood,
  And shall from age to age endure.

Psalm C.

B EFORE Jehovah's awful throne
'Ye nations bow with sacred joy,
Know that the Lord is God alone,
    He can create, and He destroy.

His sovereign power, without our aid,
    Made us of clay and formed us men:
And when like wandering sheep we strayed,
    He brought us to His fold again.

We'll crowd Thy gates with thankful songs,
    High as the heavens our voices raise:
And earth, with her ten thousand tongues,
    Shall fill Thy courts with sounding praise.

Wide as the world is Thy command:
    Vast as eternity Thy love:
Firm as a rock Thy truth shall stand,
    When rolling years shall cease to move.

The Name of Jesus.

Hymn 324.

FARRANT.

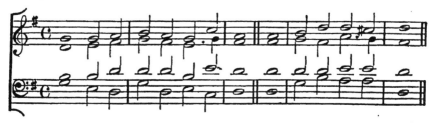

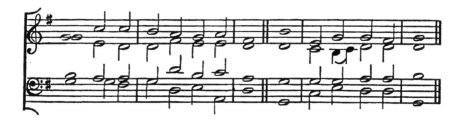

HOW sweet the Name of Jesus sounds
  In a believer's ear!
It soothes his sorrows, heals his wounds,
  And drives away his fear.

It makes the wounded spirit whole,
  And calms the troubled breast:
'Tis manna to the hungry soul,
  And to the weary rest.

Dear Name! the rock on which I build,
  My shield and hiding-place,
My never-failing treasury, filled
  With boundless stores of grace.

Jesus, my Shepherd, Husband, Friend,
  My Prophet, Priest, and King,
My Lord, my Life, my Way, my End,
  Accept the praise I bring.

Weak is the effort of my heart,
  And cold my warmest thought:
But when I see Thee as Thou art,
  I'll praise Thee as I ought.

Till then, I would my love proclaim
  With every fleeting breath;
And may the music of Thy Name
  Refresh my soul in death.

Jerusalem the Golden.

HYMN ON HEAVEN.

JERUSALEM the golden,
  With milk and honey blest,
Beneath thy contemplation
  Sink heart and voice opprest.
I know not, O I know not,
  What joys await us there,
What radiancy of glory,
  What light beyond compare.

They stand, those halls of Sion,
  All jubilant with song,
And bright with many an angel,
  And all the martyr throng.
The Prince is ever with them,
  The daylight is serene,
The pastures of the blessed
  Are decked in glorious sheen.

There is the Throne of David,
  And there, from care released,
The shouts of them that triumph,
  The song of them that feast;
And they who, with their Leader,
  Have conquered in the fight,
For ever and for ever
  Are clad in robes of white.

Nearer, my God, to Thee.

Hymn 326.

NEARER, my God, to Thee,
  Nearer to Thee :
E'en though it be a cross
  That raiseth me ;
Still all my song shall be,
Nearer, my God, to Thee,
  Nearer to Thee !

Though like a wanderer,
    The sun gone down,
Darkness comes over me,
    My rest a stone ;
Yet in my dreams I'd be
Nearer, my God, to Thee,
    Nearer to Thee !

There let my way appear
    Steps unto heaven,
All that Thou sendest me
    In mercy given ;
Angels to beckon me
Nearer, my God, to Thee,
    Nearer to Thee !

Then with my waking thoughts
    Bright with Thy praise,
Out of my stony griefs
    Bethels I'll raise :
So by my vows to be
Nearer, my God, to Thee,
    Nearer to Thee !

And when on joyful wing
    Cleaving the sky,
Sun, moon, and stars forgot,
    Upwards I fly ;
Still all my song shall be,
Nearer, my God, to Thee,
    Nearer to Thee !

The various Editions of the Year of Praise.

I. LARGE TYPE, WITH MUSIC.
Imperial 16mo., price 3s. 6d.

II. SMALL TYPE, WITH MUSIC.
Small Crown 8vo., price 1s. 6d.

III. LARGE TYPE, WITHOUT MUSIC.
Small 8vo., price 1s.

IV. SMALL TYPE, WITHOUT MUSIC.
Demy 18mo., price 6d.

ALEXANDER STRAHAN, PUBLISHER,
56, LUDGATE HILL, LONDON.